The QUIET REVOLUTION

The QUIET REVOLUTION

Reflections on the Changing Profile of American Business

ROBERT G. DUNLOP

CHILTON BOOK COMPANY

RADNOR, PENNSYLVANIA

338.0973
D922

Library of Congress Cataloging in Publication Data

Dunlop, Robert G.
  The quiet revolution.

  Includes bibliographical references.
  1. United States—Commerce. 2. Business. 3. Industry—Social aspects—
United States. I. Title.
HF5343.D85 1975   338'.0973   74-31387
ISBN 0-8019-6246-3

Foreword

Robert G. Dunlop has devoted his professional life to the management of the Sun Oil Company, and *The Quiet Revolution* embodies his conviction that there have been extraordinary changes in the business and industrial community during the past decades which parallel the extraordinary changes in American economic and social life. These changes have gone largely unnoticed and unappreciated by the general public.

He reminds us that businesses—especially those firms with alert management—have decentralized, democratized, and humanized themselves. They have moved away from a purely hierarchical pattern of organization. Firms now respond more to the changing needs of their employees and to the changes and growth of the community at large. Executives respond to such expectations as those of environmental protection or employment of groups neglected in the past.

Robert Dunlop cautions, however, that "we are demanding more from our business system at the same time that we are limiting its ability to deliver." He reminds us that if business becomes so restricted that it no longer has the incentive to try to generate wealth, "there will be little for society to share." Thus there is a necessary reciprocity implied in Dunlop's thesis; that is, as business becomes increasingly aware of its obligations to the society in which it functions, the public—consumers, government officials, and analysts—must become aware of the necessary ways that business generates wealth rather than stay mired in antiquated misconceptions.

One of the themes that Robert Dunlop develops is that of the changing meaning of work. After work has satisfied the basic needs for food and shelter, people become interested in and concerned about the nature of their work; they seek stimulus, responsibility, flexibility, and personal value in it. He believes that individuals and organizations alike benefit from the new business ideal that seeks to "alter the work rather than the worker." And he speaks approvingly of the work ethic evolving into a life ethic.

It is to this view that I would like to address myself, for Robert Dunlop himself represents an epitome of the transformed work ethic. He is devoted to human freedom, hard work, self-discipline, spiritual values, and individual growth. Indeed *The Quiet Revolution* reveals that he is committed to an ethic that brings together vocation and avocation, business and learning, in its respect for the worth of individual endeavor in society. He has devoted himself not only to the affairs of the Sun Oil Company but also to those of his alma mater, the University of Pennsylvania. And he believes in the value and power of education precisely because he believes in the development of all individual capabilities. His concept of freedom is not that of every man for himself nor merely that of freedom against external restraint or freedom to be left alone. Quite the contrary; he believes in the freedom to achieve as much as one is innately capable of achieving.

Thus Robert Dunlop asserts that the private enterprise system, to which he has devoted a lifetime of reflection and action, rests on "two closely related supports: One is a system of fundamental political beliefs that provides a high degree of freedom and opportunity for the individual while constraining the power of government. And the second is an enduring commitment to providing educational opportunities for all."

It is thus his belief in equal opportunity that causes him to be devoted to education and to business alike. Business helps the individual to develop as well as causing the country to develop. He writes, for example, of the developmental manager, the business leader, as one who is constantly concerned that the individuals under his supervision grow. The manager to be successful must open-mindedly perceive human interaction as a dynamic process whereby the manager learns what risks he can take individually and how others can be taught craftsmanship and self-discipline. Characteristically, Robert Dunlop regards the manager as one who starts changes: "Above all, he grows, and provides room for others to grow."

Growth requires a sense of self-discipline. A business manager must be "goal-oriented" and manage "resources with an eye to continuity, even when tomorrow's needs require sacrificing today's advantage." Businessmen and women must "demonstrate a greater sense of personal accountability for the actions of [their] organizations." A disciplined, professional, and humane attitude toward work and the provision of work opportunities pervades the volume. And it is not surprising that Robert Dunlop in his conclusion calls for the nation to recommit itself to the old values of belief in a Creator, belief in life under law, and belief in the brotherhood of man. He believes our nation needs a "recommitment to a set of moral values that has been the root of our strength in the past . . . a blend of the concepts of love, humility, justice, compassion, trust, and responsibility. These are the qualities that are the essence of productive day-to-day relationships among people."

Robert Dunlop's reflections on his life in business represent the democratic and moral heritage of this nation, for he finds his trust in a reliance on the possibilities of human nature and a faith in human intelligence. He believes that the nation can grow and that people can grow. Faith in God-given human potentialities is thus a way of using and developing all human resources, whether they be those in business or the university.

I am fortunate to be able to call Robert Dunlop a colleague and friend, for I have seen him demonstrate what he believes. His way of life has seen him devoted to the University of Pennsylvania as well as to his firm, his family, and his friends. I wish our world had more such men and women.

MARTIN MEYERSON
President
University of Pennsylvania

Preface

In what directions has U.S. business been moving in these recent decades of sweeping change? What is the role of business in helping to meet America's pressing social problems? Can—and should—our economy continue to grow? Regarding energy, specifically, what is the genesis of today's scarcities, and what is required for a strengthened U.S. fuels position in the future?

These are the questions that I have attempted to address in reflecting on my four decades of experience in the petroleum industry. I have enjoyed many opportunities over the years to discuss these matters with my Sun associates and with others in industry, and to benefit from the thinking of those in the academic community who are specially concerned with business. I am deeply indebted to all for helping to broaden my understanding. And for their ideas and insights that are reflected in these observations, I here express my appreciation. The conclusions reflect my own views, rather than those of Sun Oil Company, and my personal philosophy; any shortcomings that may exist are mine.

I gratefully acknowledge the assistance of many associates in Sun Oil Company in bringing these thoughts together in this form. Particularly, I thank Miss Dorothy M. Stewart, my personal secretary; Mrs. Judy Downes, who typed and proofed this text; and Dean S. Chaapel, who has provided continuing editorial assistance to me in the preparation of my public statements.

ROBERT G. DUNLOP
1974

Contents

Prologue

THE ECONOMIC ADVANCE OF THE UNITED STATES in the twentieth century is without precedent in the history of the world. In the past four decades alone, since the depth of the Great Depression, the value of the nation's output of goods and services (in constant dollars) has increased sixfold and per capita disposable personal income has risen by more than three times.

With only 7 percent of the world's land area and just 6 percent of its people, the United States now accounts for one-third of the world's production of basic goods and services.

The result for Americans is an unmatched level of physical affluence and a steadily improving quality of life.

Reflecting that affluence are these facts: Two of every three American families own their own homes;

eight in ten own at least one automobile. The proportion enjoying the use of labor-saving and convenience appliances far exceeds that of any other people. And supporting this level of living is a U.S. per capita energy consumption rate that is almost six times the world average.

Not so susceptible of numerical measurement, but perhaps of even greater significance, is the improving quality of life in this country. Major improvements include a steadily lengthening life expectancy, resulting from advances in medicine and health care; a rich and growing variety of educational opportunities available to a rising proportion of the population; a broadening national commitment to preserving the environment; and expanding programs of assistance to the disadvantaged, the disabled, the elderly and others in need.

In this first half of the decade of the 1970s, a record-high 85 million people hold jobs; goods and services are being produced at an annual rate of $1.4 trillion; and median family income is more than $12,000 per year.

The principal thrust behind this economic and social progress is the American private enterprise business system composed of more than 12 million firms large and small across the land. At the base of the system's achievements are the capabilities of the working men and women who give those companies substance and form, the investors who provide the capital essential to growth, the entrepreneurs and managers who assume risks and provide direction, and the innovation and technological advancement that spring from the marriage of human talent and capital resources.

This private enterprise system and its achievements rest, in turn, upon two closely related supports. One is a system of fundamental political beliefs that provides a high degree of freedom and opportunity for the individual while constraining the power of government. And the second is an enduring commitment to providing educational opportunities for all, a commitment which has in many ways made possible the continuing political stability and economic advancement of America.

Enter here the grand paradoxes. Our country's dissatisfaction with its unfinished work rises in step with its material progress. And its business system, credited with achieving preeminence in the living standards of its people, falls in esteem at the moment it is being asked to shoulder new responsibilities.

According to the Daniel Yankelovich research organization, two of every three Americans were saying last year that business has "too much power" and should be regulated to protect consumers and the national interest.

These attitudes reflect in part the fact that discontents are natural and normal in a growing and changing society where the expectations of people are rising. But they also reflect the inability of American business, particularly large corporations, to communicate to the public in an understandable way the facts about their enterprises, what they are doing, and how they do it. The truth is that revolutionary change in American economic and social life in recent decades has been accompanied by revolutionary change in the business community. But this has been a quiet revolution, not the stuff of which headlines are made.

And the public continues to think of business as operating now in the same fashion as it did 50 to 75 years ago.

But an awareness of change is essential to informed public appraisal of business performance. So the following observations focus on what I have seen happening in American business in the past 40 years.

Part I

——*——

THE CHANGING PROFILE

CHAPTER 1

---*---

New Perspectives in Management

> Business life in the 1950-1970 period became
> more decentralized, diverse and personalized.
> The fundamental reasons for this were the
> increasing dependence of business on innovation
> and on the highly personal qualities of knowl-
> edge and the ability to communicate. Such im-
> personal elements of business as physical assets
> were still important—and would continue to be
> —but the corporation as a community was no
> longer modeled on the machine, designed from
> above for a single specific purpose with each cog
> performing its appointed task.[1]

THOSE words from *Fortune* magazine capture the
essence of the changing profile of American business.

At the heart of this change, which continues at an
accelerated pace today, are a number of closely related
developments that have been interacting over a long

period to alter the basic make-up of the U.S. corporation. Chief among them are the emergence of a new breed of career managers, the evolution of a new philosophy of management and a new style of managing, new concepts of organization, new tools and techniques and a new approach to communication.

In one way or another, all of these changes reflect the response of business to a steadily changing environment. The growing complexity of external forces impacting upon business operations increased tremendously the scope and difficulty of the management job. The need for specialized knowledge and specialists grew rapidly. And the ability of individual owner-entrepreneurs, no matter how gifted, to effectively direct sizable and growing enterprises correspondingly declined.

I was privileged to assist in bridging this gap between the older and the newer management approaches, since my service as president and chairman of Sun Oil Company ranged from the period of direct executive control by members of the founding Pew family through a major merger to the complete reorganization of the company at the close of the 1960s.

Throughout that period, the complexity of management in the petroleum industry increased at an astounding rate. The physical volume of operations increased many times over as U.S. demand for energy rose steadily. New technology revolutionized refining. Oil finding and recovery techniques were reshaped by scientific advances. International operations were sharply expanded, with all the attendant considerations of world finance and international diplomatic

4

relationships. Change such as this in petroleum and other industries literally demanded a new approach to management.

And that change came in the emergence of career managers, or management specialists, who were not major owners of the firms they directed.

Earlier, this "management revolution" had been anticipated as a major threat to the future of U.S. business. Back in the 1930s, for example, some observers argued that under hired managers, who owned only infinitesimal shares of their companies, corporations would no longer be run with the objective of maximizing profit. Risk-takers would give way to bureaucrats with no interest in innovation and growth, the argument ran. And, ultimately, business would stagnate.

Obviously, this has not occurred. Rather, as stock ownership has broadened in recent decades, there has been increasing pressure on management to maximize performance. As one chief executive puts it, the economists who say that today's corporate manager no longer feels pressure for earnings performance should try coming home to face the cleaning woman who owns 10 shares of his company's stock and wants to know if she should buy more.

William Letwin, of the Sloan School at Massachusetts Institute of Technology, makes this further point:

> It is reassuring to observe . . . that today's managers show the same vigorous appetite for income and wealth that spurred yesterday's businessmen to bold progress. Moreover, the earnings of executives, especially their earnings in the form of stock options, tend to turn the success-

ful executive into an owner himself, thus giving
him a powerful incentive to harmonize his interests as manager and owner; in other words, making him act like a traditional entrepreneurial
businessman.[2]

In Sun Oil Company, for example, employee ownership is encouraged at all levels through a stock pur-
chase plan going back almost 50 years, while a management performance share plan relates executive
compensation in part to the increase in return on
shareholders equity over a period of time. In my
view, these plans contribute significantly to a blending of employee-owner interests.

The assembling of professional or career management teams to handle an increasingly complex task of
managing has been accompanied by related changes in
business organization and in management philosophy
and style.

Traditionally, the organizational patterns of American business have been characterized by a series of
pyramids peaking in the chief executive. The typical
structure was highly centralized, featuring tightly controlled operations and an authoritarian management
style. And it proved itself over a period of many years
to be highly stable and well-suited to handling regular
on-going operations with a high degree of efficiency.

But in more recent years, as a changing environment brought new external pressures to bear on business, that traditional structure proved to be sluggish
and unresponsive. Its strengths proved, in rapidly
changing circumstances, to be its weaknesses. The
fatal weakness was its tendency to discourage creativity and experimentation.

New forms of organization then began to evolve. And today organizational change ranges all the way from minor surgery on the pyramidal pattern to Robert Townsend's admonition in *Up the Organization* to throw out organization charts altogether because they "strangle profit and stifle people."

New concepts in organization in business carry such descriptive designations as "bottom-up," "project," and "beehive" management. Most feature a number of common characteristics, starting with the basic concept that people have a broad grant of authority within which to act for the organization. Importantly, they are alike in pushing decision-making authority down to low levels. And what they achieve is not only a loosening of the structure to give it greater speed and flexibility, but an environment that encourages people to develop their capabilities.

The real force behind such change is the desire to remove organizational restraints that stifle initiative and to make the organization itself a force for innovation through the release of human potential.

We had direct experience with this several years ago in Sun Oil Company, when a merger provided the opportunity to develop a completely new organizational structure. In designing it, we sought to take full advantage of the motivation potential. One of our basic thrusts, for example, was a broad decentralization of the structure, moving authority and decision-making to the level of direct involvement with the problem. And we found that so delegating authority helped to build a climate in which individuals are challenged to become more deeply involved in their work and to develop and grow in managerial competence and effectiveness. The organizational structure itself, in this case, is proving to be a positive motivational force.

As traditional organization patterns have been altered, the approach to management and the style of managing have undergone perhaps even greater change.

In the past, the general approach to management was characterized by a kind of authoritarianism that flowed downward naturally through the pyramidal organization structure. It was marked by rigid policies and procedures that are reflected in such positions as "this must be cleared through me."

In recent years, however, a sharply different managerial style has been evolving. Variously referred to as participative, democratic or developmental, it is rooted in a completely different set of attitudes. Max Ways in *Fortune* has referred to it as the "you don't need me, do you?" style, going on to say:

> Within the corporation, top managers are less and less inclined to view themselves as the prime fonts of judgment, decision and policy. The men at the top are more and more concerned with encouraging horizontal flows of information among the parts of the organization so that the left hand will know when the right hand's thumb is in a wringer.[3]

While this new style of managing is still being analyzed and defined, our experience in Sun Oil Company tells us that it has some very specific characteristics. The developmental manager is open-minded. He is accessible and easy to talk to. He shares information, and he perceives communication as a continuing process rather than an intermittent activity. He is an informed risk-taker. He learns from mistakes and helps others to do so. He sets high standards and challenging goals. He gives credit commensurate with performance. He is goal-oriented and helps others to be so. He is attuned to change and an initiator of change. And, above all, he grows, and provides room for others to grow. One of my colleagues caught the essence of the concept, it seems to me, when he called the developmental manager a "creative activist."

Along with changing structures and styles, the introduction of new management tools and techniques, including those that are lumped under the label of "management science," are also helping to reshape the profile of business.

Courtney C. Brown of Columbia University has commented that what has really been happening in the application of new management tools is an extension of human brain power through mathematics and electronic systems of rapid computation and of storage and retrieval of vast amounts of information.

At the heart of this extension is the computer and its satellite equipment. And already, these facilities are performing varied data processing and other activities in both financial and operational areas.

In a broader sense, the use of computer models, operations research techniques and other systems approaches have begun to contribute to more-informed and systematic decision-making by managers. Their particular value lies in identifying alternative courses of action and in helping to establish priorities, for these are hard processes in which decision-makers need all the help they can get.

Contrary to earlier fears, the utilization of these new tools and techniques is not threatening to dehumanize management. For they are aids to people rather than substitutes for people. And there continue to be factors of judgment, experience and intuition—a feel for the market—that cannot be programmed into a computer. The hard responsibility of decision-making comes to rest ultimately on people. And I suspect that most chief executive officers would agree with Harry Truman's terse appraisal that "the buck stops here."

It seems to me also that the major contributions of management science to better administration and decision-making are still to come. C. Jackson Grayson of Southern Methodist University has suggested that an overconcern with theory and methodology has limited the practical application of management science aids and has called upon both managers and management scientists to start building better bridges between the two fields. An effort to gain common recognition of the fact that knowing what to count is fully as important as knowing how to count it might be a good place to start.

Part and parcel of these organizational and management changes is the evolution of a new concept of communication in business. It would be overstating the case to say that truly effective communication has been realized within the typical corporate community. But progress toward real communication is being made. And it reflects a belated recognition by business that communication is the process *central* to success in any undertaking involving large numbers of people. As a result, businesses today are sharing more information *and* working to remove the barriers —barriers of organization, status, language, change resistance—that prohibit communication.

Peter Drucker has said that real communication requires "shared experience in decisions"—and that without such experience there is no way that people can gain the common perceptions that are the basis for understanding. It is my observation that changes in structure and style today are creating the kind of environment in which individuals and groups can share the experience of establishing goals and reaching decisions. And the improved communication that is resulting is one of the growing strengths of business for the future.

The interaction of these changes has quietly reshaped American business, producing a new thrust and vitality that are far removed from the image that persists in the public eye. The public appears to see business in old stereotypes. That image is one of a few order-givers and many order-takers with the latter working in a tightly controlled structure that denies even their right to question why. And it persists, perhaps, because of the tendency of many, both outside and inside business, to talk about today's organizations in the same terms that were used to describe vastly different enterprises many years ago.

Business today is more personal, more flexible, more attuned to change and more responsive to the needs of people both within the organization and in the society in which it exists. It has adapted to a changing environment and to changing demands upon it. And

11

in doing so, it has sustained and strengthened an economic thrust that is without parallel in history.

John Mee of Indiana University has expressed the essence of this change and its impact in these words:

> Both economic growth and the development of management philosophy have progressed in comparable stages in the same period of time. The managers in the United States have been the coalescing forces in the achievement of predetermined economic and social objectives . . . they have had the advantage of a developing management philosophy that has enabled the practice of management to become an art of discriminating analysis and creative synthesis for utilizing the products of technology for the benefit of organized society.[4]

CHAPTER 2

———✳———

Changing Concepts of People and Work

THE emergence of "human resources" as a working phrase in the language and literature of American business symbolizes a major change in the corporation's relationships with people. For those words encompass fresh ideas of human potential, work, job design, and personal interaction that are shaping a new direction in industrial progress.

In many ways, these new ideas are an outgrowth of new management perspectives; they closely reflect the opening up of the organizational structure and the birth of a new management philosophy and a new managerial style. The result is an approach to managing people and work that recognizes and responds to a challenge once voiced by David E.

13

Lilienthal, former chairman of the Atomic Energy Commission, in these words:

> The greatest of all resources, the indispensable ones, are the energies of individuals. Therefore, it is a key task of managerial leadership to recognize the existence of these often unused or partially used human talents, energies and imagination. The full release of human energy is the central purpose and function of the manager at all levels. . . .[1]

In moving to meet that challenge, American business is creating relationships with employees that are vastly different from those which existed in the earlier decades of this century, even though those tend to persist in the public eye.

In earlier years, the growth of the mass market and the development of mass production techniques to serve it focused management attention on work specialization, speed and efficiency. The individual worker and his working situation received limited consideration. And the result was that human abilities were badly underutilized, to the disadvantage of both individuals and organizations.

In many respects, this situation in business reflected social values that were deeply rooted in master-servant relationships extending back to the earliest days of recorded history.

But at the same time that business was reflecting the older values of society, it was also becoming a major contributor to social change, especially through the spawning of a new "middle class" and of the technology that was to profoundly influence American culture. Increased productivity promoted wealth,

14

and wealth promoted independence and a growing concern for human development. These changing social values were, in turn, reflected in business. And from such continuing interaction came new values and new relationships.

In the past, business leaders have been quick to say that the people of their organizations were their most important resource. I have said as much myself. But it has been only in relatively recent years that priority efforts have been devoted to the effective development and utilization of the skills of people. And it is this somewhat different precept that is at the base of a new management commitment to conducting the business in a way that enables people to fully use their capabilities and creativity in attaining organizational goals.

This commitment reflects the recognition by business of two basic principles. First is the growing realization that a satisfying work situation is the key to a satisfying and useful life. Albert Camus once expressed it this way: "Without work, all life goes rotten. But when work is soulless, life stifles and dies."

Second is the recognition that a satisfying work situation enables people to perform at full potential, with a resultant strengthening of the productivity and competitive stance of the organization.

The new philosophy of people and work has evolved very slowly, and only in recent years has it impacted substantially on policy and organization. But it is beginning to shape new approaches to the conduct and operations of business. And in many ways, it promises to be the most revolutionary of all forces now at work in American business.

15

Particularly significant in the new relationships being shaped today are these three aspects of change: Change in the corporate approach to managing people, change in the way work is regarded and jobs are designed, and change flowing from the advance in knowledge and technology.

The first of these is reflected in developments in Sun Oil Company over the past decade. Sun has traditionally been closely concerned with the welfare of employees, providing a high degree of job security, high levels of compensation and generous employee benefit programs. And it has enjoyed a very favorable reputation as a place to work, and harmonious relationships with employees.

At the same time, however, the company was also characterized by a somewhat rigid organizational structure and by traditions which tended to build walls around avenues of advancement open to employees.

As the company grew and as the external environment became more complex and competitive pressures intensified, it became apparent that the past approach to managing people and work was limiting both individual and organizational opportunities for development and growth. So, during the 1960s, the company began to move toward a new concept of relationships with employees—a move which was accelerated by the change accompanying a major merger.

Key to this new approach was the adoption of a human resources policy intended to place more responsibility for initiative on each individual, while at the same time providing an environment in which initiative may be exercised. The objective is to create an organizational environment conducive to developing and utilizing the talents of every employee to the maximum extent possible. At the heart of the new philosophy is a conviction that people, if they really are the most valuable asset of business, should be developed with greater care than any other resource.

This approach requires that managers allocate time and energy *to increasing the value of the human assets* under their direction, an activity for which little or no incentive was provided in earlier years. And that leads to some concrete benefits, which British management consultants E. J. Singer and John Ramsden have expressed this way:

> Thinking about people as a capital asset . . . would focus management thinking on the long-term development and use of this precious resource . . . managers will be encouraged to make the best use of human resources. They will be encouraged to think about job enrichment, about using people to the limit of their capacities, about wasting potential.[2]

An 11-point policy statement expressing Sun's philosophy very clearly places on management and managers the responsibility for creating the kind of working climate that will permit individual employees to assume responsibility for their share of the total objectives of the organization. It makes the development of people as a corporate resource a part of the job of every manager, and holds him accountable for it. It makes individual development and growth a part of each employee's job responsibility. It emphasizes the need for flexibility and mobility in permitting and encouraging people to move from one part of the organization to another, or from one career path to another. And it pledges that "each employee shall receive individual consideration and recognition and the opportunity for planned self-improvement and achievement. . . ."

In brief, the policy is designed to guide management toward the goal of achieving growth for every individual in the organization.

A second major thrust for change in business-employee relationships has been the emergence of basic questions about past approaches to work and job design.

Evidence has been accumulating for years that many people at all organizational levels are in some ways dissatisfied with their work and working situations. Many say their work is boring and repetitive, others say that it lacks challenge and others say that it is unfulfilling. The "blue collar blues" became a familiar refrain some years ago; and more recently, white-collar and professional people have indicated that they share these frustrations. Closer examination of the problem indicates that dissatisfactions relate not only to individual jobs but extend to the nature of work itself.

As evidence that the work ethic is going out of style, observers cite growing absenteeism in industry, increasing resistance to overtime work, the earlier retirement of white-collar employees and executives and the growing refusal of people to accept jobs that they see as menial or unpleasant.

The fact that there is widespread discontent with work situations and severe job-related tensions today is without question. But this does not necessarily reflect a widespread alienation from work. For the other side of this coin is that more than 90 percent of men in their prime working years are, in fact, at work. A rising proportion of women are in the labor market and hold jobs. Surveys show that large percentages of those on welfare would rather be working if they could find a job. And some 80 percent of young people say that they feel that commitment to a career is essential in life.

What has been happening, it seems to me, is not that people are valuing work *less* but they are valuing it differently. Or, to put it another way, the work ethic has been undergoing a major transition. And the nature of the transition has been aptly expressed by a labor official who suggests that "maybe we ought to stop talking about the work ethic and start talking about the life ethic."

The transition reflects in part a phenomenon that researchers have referred to as "the hierarchy of needs." This holds simply that man is concerned first with satisfying basic needs that are essential to life and living. When these needs are met, he focuses on higher-order needs, moving progressively up the scale as he satisfies succeeding wants. In these terms, work is performed first for survival. Then, as a major share of basic desires are satisfied through steadily rising wages and benefits, man turns his attention to still higher-level needs. Today, people are concerned about the nature of the work they do in terms of meaningfulness and psychic satisfaction.

This comes through very clearly in the career goals expressed by young people. For example, surveys on career motivation have reported that 8 out of 10 students say they want a job in which they can make a contribution to society. Commenting on this, S. I. Hayakawa has expressed this view:

> The traditional rewards of work are not going to be enough . . . many people are going to want aesthetic satisfaction . . . self-expression. They are going to want ethical satisfaction, a belief in the value of what they are doing, a conviction that their efforts will contribute to the needs of society.[3]

The past preoccupation of business with the mechanics of production has contributed to present frustrations through denying to many the opportunity for meaningful involvement in their work.

H. Robert Sharbaugh, Sun Oil president and my associate in management, has graphically described the resulting problem by pointing up the tendency for jobs to be built in the form of "little boxes." He comments:

> The lines of those little boxes signal to the people inside that the scope of their work and responsibility is rather rigidly limited, and that involvement beyond those limits is neither encouraged nor welcomed nor rewarded . . . this effectively blocks off real involvement in work, and the gains that flow from such involvement. A basic part of our task now is to erase the lines around those little boxes and to develop a new way of thinking about people at work—and to raise our expectations about what people can, and will, and want to do.[4]

And American business is beginning to do precisely that, by embracing new concepts of job design that seek to alter the work rather than the worker.

A variety of approaches to enriching and enlarging jobs are being tested and applied today with excellent results. They are basically designed to provide opportunities for the fuller use of individual capabilities, and they involve changes like these:

They seek to give the employee a module of work and to build into it direct, personal responsibility. They involve the employee in decision-making about his job, including how his work is organized. They provide recognition for the contribution of each individual job to the overall accomplishments of the organization. They assign work to teams rather than to individuals. They allow people to participate in establishing their own working hours and working conditions. They look at facility design as a consideration in job involvement and work motivation. They foster direct, personal and continuing communication. And they involve management style and organizational design that are geared to encouraging the creativity of people.

A number of companies in diverse fields have achieved a high degree of success in applying these new approaches. M. Scott Myers, who pioneered in job enrichment programs at Texas Instruments, has identified such individual and organizational gains as improved attitudes and team efforts, reduced anxiety, the unleashing of new ideas, more open communication, reduced costs and increased productivity.

A third source of change is the thrust of expanding knowledge and developing technology, which are sharply altering the approach to work and jobs. No longer can the American industrial scene be accurately depicted by the earlier stereotypes of robot-like work-

21

ers on factory assembly lines. The factory is no longer the typical American workplace; the proportion of people in manufacturing continues to decline as employment rises in transportation, utilities, trade and other fields. And contrary to the popular notion, fewer than 2 percent of employed Americans work on assembly lines today.

New technology and a steadily changing business mix are moving America from a manufacturing to a service economy and creating a vast variety of new occupations and jobs. This has created a growing demand for what Peter Drucker refers to as "knowledge workers," or people who work with their minds. And as a result, an increasing proportion of Americans hold jobs that truly challenge their capabilities.

The essence of the rich variety of change that has been occurring in the relationship of American business to its people is the growing recognition of the primary importance of the individual human being to the organization. Work and jobs are being increasingly personalized, and both individuals and organizations are benefitting.

There is a far way to go to reach the point where the majority of Americans find their work truly satisfying and fully stimulating. For some types of work simply are not susceptible to such change, just as some people may have no wish to be so challenged. But the road is opening to a revolutionary reshaping of work for most Americans, as the roadblocks to satisfaction and involvement are steadily removed.

Scott Myers, drawing on his broad industrial and academic experience, summarizes the situation this way:

22

Changing Concepts of People and Work

Today's manager finds himself in a ground-swell of a quiet revolution . . . the challenge of increasing human effectiveness is emerging as the remaining frontier, offering competitive advantage to organizations most successful in channeling human talent and energy into constructive outlets. . . . Tomorrow's manager will manage through the influence of competence, organizing materiel and manpower to give expression to talent and individuality in the pursuit of synergistic personal and organizational goals.[5]

CHAPTER 3

————※————

External Challenge and Response

A SWELLING WAVE of new public demands has created sharp challenges for America's institutions in the past decade.

Pressures on government, business and other institutions for preserving the environment, protecting consumers and expanding opportunities for the under-privileged reflect the rising expectations of the American people for an improved quality of life. Business has been especially affected, because these pressures have added a new social dimension to its traditional tasks of producing goods and services and providing jobs.

The breadth of the challenge has been pointed up by the Daniel Yankelovich research organization in these words:

> . . . (these pressures) have the potential to exert
> a major impact on virtually all of a corporation's

24

operations: the degree of autonomy under which the corporation functions; the shape of future corporate goals and plans; current profitability; and the all important area of the company's reputation. . . .[1]

The effort to understand and interpret these pressures, to establish priorities for response and to respond in productive ways has broadened the scope of corporate decision-making and substantially increased the complexity of corporate management.

A major difficulty in responding is the existence of inherent contradictions in many of the emerging public demands. For example, the public wants more energy; but at the same time, it restricts the development of that energy because of concern over environmental damage. Again, the public wants higher standards in product servicing; but its concern for controlling prices indicates that it doesn't want to bear the costs involved.

A part of the problem is that traditional ideology has delayed direct action on some problems. And this has fostered the growth of special interest groups that have pushed hard for objectives of their own, with little concern for balanced responses to the broader problems.

Nonetheless, where specific new demands can be identified from these shifting external pressures, business is responding. This involves both voluntary action and compliance with new laws and regulations. And significant change in the perspectives of business is resulting.

The broadest challenges have stemmed from consumerism and the drive for environmental improvement. What has been happening in these areas is representative of the nature of the new external pressures and of business's response to them.

At the heart of consumerism, public opinion surveys report, is the feeling of 5 out of 10 Americans that they are highly vulnerable to irresponsible business tactics in the areas of product quality and safety, advertising and follow-through servicing. These views are widespread among the affluent and well-educated, as well as among lower-income and less-educated groups.

In regard to the environment, the public holds business primarily responsible for air and water pollution. Further, 7 people in 10 say business is doing too little to deal with the problem, with the majority looking to government to force business action.

Without question, these public concerns reflect real problems that have impacted on individuals. But it is also true that they reflect significant economic and social change in America. In this sense, they are really an outgrowth of industrial progress, for it is this progress that has provided the economic security and the broadened educational experience that have resulted in large numbers of people turning their attention to the quality of life and living.

Although similar in origin, consumerism and environmentalism differ in other ways, with each posing its own set of response problems for business.

Consumerism, for example, is not a new phenomenon. Philip Kotler of Northwestern University identifies the current activity as the third consumer movement in America, following earlier confrontations in the early 1900s and in the mid-1930s. Both of the earlier movements were marked by resistance to rising prices and by fairly specific issues such as food and drug problems. Both were also essentially temporary in nature, ending in new or expanded federal regulatory action to protect consumer interests.

Today's consumerism is proving to be something quite different, although recognition of this was slow in developing. The difference lies not so much in the issues—rising prices and product safety are still concerns—as in basic change in the individual's situation as a buyer.

At the base of this change is the steady advance in American technology and the resulting proliferation of new products and improvements and refinements in older products. These advances have confronted consumers with a broad range of choice, a widening knowledge gap and considerable frustration in choosing. E. B. Weiss, a verteran observer of advertising and marketing trends, depicts the consumer's dilemma this way:

> Technology has brought unparalleled abundance and opportunity to the consumer. It has also exposed him to new complexities and hazards. It has made his choices more difficult. He cannot be chemist, mechanic, electrician, nutritionist and a walking computer. Faced with almost infinite product differentiation (plus contrived product virtues that are purely semantic), considerable price differentiation, the added complexities of trading stamps, the subtleties of cents-off deals and other complications, the shopper is expected to choose wisely under circumstances that baffle professional buyers.[2]

27

Business was slow to perceive this crisis of complexity and the depth of consumer discontent with advertising and servicing. So it was slow to react. And consumer issues were increasingly pushed into the national spotlight by the growing attention of Congress and the Executive Branch, Ralph Nader's crusade for auto safety and the upsurge in activist groups. The interplay of these forces culminated in the major thrust of consumerism that continues today, and that promises to be a permanent fixture in business-customer relations.

The slow response of business, in my opinion, was largely due to a widespread feeling that it was *already* operating, and long had been, in the best interests of consumers. Business people, after all, cut their teeth on the knowledge that a firm is successful only when it produces products and services that people want to buy. They were aware, also, that responsible business enterprises have long stressed product quality. And they knew, too, that the discipline of the market, coupled with government regulation, was advancing the interests of consumers long before consumerism became the popular concept it is today.

At the same time, one other dimension of the consumer movement was giving business serious pause. This was the view advanced by some that business should produce not what the consumer wants, but what will be good for him. This has an attractive sound in the theoretical sense, but it doesn't sell in the real world.

Deciding what consumers *shall have* in a market where free choice may be exercised is beyond the power of even the largest businesses. One has only to recall the disaster of the Edsel motor car to be vividly reminded that an established name brand and extensive advertising and promotion will not make a success of a product that too few want.

This is not to say that the role of business should be purely passive in catering to consumer tastes. Its technical knowledge and ability to command exceptional talent in many areas of specialization should be applied to lead consumer choice toward optimum values in design, utility, durability, safety and other features which represent true quality. Pity, however, the business that attempts to lead as far and as fast as some theoreticians of what is good for consumers might wish!

When all this has been said, however, the fact remains that the actions—and inactions—of business in many ways invited the aggressive behavior of the consumer movement. Among the trouble spots were advertising excesses, failure to assure the availability of adequate product servicing, failure to provide the kind of information essential to comparison shopping, an indifferent response to complaints and a lethargic response to what consumers were saying.

Belatedly, however, business has begun to listen. On balance, it is responding positively in ways that strengthen the position of the buyer and increase product satisfaction.

Basic to this response is the emergence of a new business stance that sees consumerism as an opportunity for building better relations and expanding markets. Flowing naturally from this approach are new programs designed to meet the consumer's prime needs of more and better information and direct assistance when problems develop.

Programs to provide information needed for intelligent buying decisions are widespread. They include campaigns to tell people what to consider in buying cars and appliances, provision of unit pricing information, improved labeling, making instructional booklets available, and inclusion in advertisements of information useful in appraising performance.

Increasingly, this new approach is being reflected in organizational change designed to make business more responsive to consumer needs. New departments in many companies today are concerned with consumer affairs, product quality, customer relations and advertising review. And while some of these efforts may be cosmetic, most represent effectively functioning groups enjoying a high-level corporate commitment and direct access to executive management.

A recent National Industrial Conference Board survey of 149 large companies with full-time consumer affairs departments reports that such units are helping their companies to substantially improve consumer relations. The report observes:

> . . . (consumer affairs directors) tend to regard themselves as the "voice of the consumer" in management councils. And, by positioning their consumer affairs units high in their organizations, many managements have demonstrated their wish to hear that voice.[3]

Customer relations and consumer affairs activities initiated by Sun some years ago have contributed significantly to improved relations. They have helped to reduce complaints, improve the handling of complaints and generally sensitize the company to consumer needs.

Other direct responses to consumerism include improved products such as gasolines that reduce harmful emissions, expanded dealer training activities, and programs for consumer appraisal of service and repair work.

Environmental pressures have affected business even more severely, although with a somewhat different emphasis. The public holds business heavily responsible for pollution, but not solely responsible since government and individual citizens are seen as sharing the blame. In fact, it is uniquely true that in regard to the pollution issue all are a part of the problem and all must be a part of the solution.

Pollution emerged as a major national problem in the 1960s with a suddenness that surprised virtually the entire nation. In retrospect, the failure to come to grips with the problem earlier is an indictment of American institutions generally. For the evidence of highly damaging pollution had been accumulating for some years as the population became increasingly concentrated in urban industrial areas, as industrial facilities expanded and as a growing and increasingly affluent population consumed a rising volume and variety of goods.

When the storm broke, reason gave way to emotion. And pretty well lost in the resulting confusion was the fact that many businesses had long been working to control pollution both voluntarily and in response to existing regulations. As far back as the 1930s, for example, oil companies were taking special measures to dispose of salt water encountered in drilling the East

Texas field. Throughout the industry, drilling and producing operations utilized special equipment to prevent blowouts and spills; refineries were provided with equipment to treat water used in processing and cooling; and distribution facilities included safeguards against product spills and leakage.

Despite such precautions, damaging accidents and spills have occurred—and there is no assurance that similar problems will not occur in the future. However, I think that objective analysis demonstrates that over time the petroleum industry's environmental record is a good one—not the best possible, not impossible of improvement and surely not as good as we would like it to be—but still a good one.

Indicative of the record is the industry's experience in offshore drilling and production. During the 25-year history of modern offshore operations, including the drilling of more than 17,000 wells and the production of over 5 billion barrels of oil and 24 trillion cubic feet of natural gas, there have been only four accidents involving serious pollution problems.

Other industries were similarly engaged in working to prevent or control pollution. But the total effort, lacking in coordination, technology and urgency, failed to keep pace with the rising volume of pollutants generated by a growing and increasingly consumption oriented economy. And by the late 1960s, it was painfully apparent that nobody had been doing enough to stem the rising tide of pollution and move toward resource renewal. In a relatively short time, public anxieties were transformed into new laws and rigid regulations designed to clean up our air, water and other resources.

32

A current appraisal of the national response to the environmental challenges during the past five years indicates that solid progress has been made. And the actions of business in accordance with new public policies have contributed importantly to that progress.

Perhaps the key contribution of business has been the introduction of the cost-benefit concept into the complex mix of environmental considerations. In the climate of crisis that characterized initial recognition of the scope of the U.S. pollution problem, environmental groups and legislators alike demanded the immediate adoption of exacting standards to be met within very short time-frames. Little or no attention was given to the benefits to be obtained relative to the costs to be incurred, setting the stage for a wasteful use of scarce resources in environmental overkill.

As one example, Congress passed the Air Quality Act of 1970 with tough automotive emission standards that the law said must be met regardless of costs. This not only committed the nation to tremendous expenditures for a level of emission control not required for health or other reasons, but also substantially boosted gasoline consumption. Automotive emission controls were consuming an additional 300,000 barrels daily of gasoline in 1973, with the possibility that this could rise to 2 million barrels daily by 1980, according to the office of Emergency Preparedness.

Petroleum and other businesses have continued to spearhead the fight for consideration of costs relative to benefits in environmental decisions and actions. And progress is being achieved. Significantly, John W. Tukey, head of the President's Science Advisory Committee Panel of Chemicals and Health, has recommended that future environmental legislation not set specific numerical objectives but only general goals. He pointed out that with new scientific knowledge about the health effects of pollution running up against often-inflexible old decisions, it would be unwise to set rigid standards in future legislation.

A second industry response has been the creation of new organizational units at high levels to coordinate environmental conservation activities and to reflect environmental considerations in corporate decision-making. The establishment of such a unit by Sun Oil Company several years ago has provided a capability for environmental impact analysis and early identification of problem areas, and has resulted in improved environmental planning and increased coordination of pollution-control activities.

Third, business has acted both voluntarily and in response to government initiatives on a broad front to prevent or lessen industrial pollution. The scope of change that has occurred in a few short years is virtually revolutionary for an advanced industrial society, although this appears to be little perceived by the public.

Perceived or not, the results are solid. Auto emissions have been steadily decreasing. The air in our cities is getting cleaner. Business investment in pollution control facilities is rising steadily, and expenditures for environmental research are climbing. According to the U.S. Department of Commerce, business capital outlays for air and water pollution abatement were expected to reach $6.5 billion in 1974. And governments are instituting large-scale programs to reduce pollution from sewage and solid waste.

At the same time, industry is providing leadership in the effort to achieve the critical balance between environmental and other public policies that is essential to the continuing productive growth of the U.S. economy. This is particularly significant in relation to energy policy, since environmental concerns have added to demand for fuels while restricting the development of new supplies.

In brief, business has been and is continuing to respond in productive ways to the changing environment in which it operates. This ranges beyond consumerism and environmentalism to such diverse areas as the drive for equality in employment opportunities, new concepts in industrial safety and health and a fuller accounting of business stewardship to owners and to the public.

In the broad sense, this responsiveness is reflected in the addition to corporate boards of outside directors not involved in company operations. This is bringing to bear on company policy formulation and decision making new views and perspectives that improve corporate perceptions of the outside world and its new demands on business.

In my own experience, the addition of outside directors has significantly benefitted Sun Oil Company. The broad credentials of men who have been active in government and public policy formulation, in academic research and teaching and in public affairs and communication are invaluable in helping the corporation to assess and respond to the economic and social challenges of the day.

Conversely, I feel that the addition to boards of people who represent specific constituencies, and who serve as advocates for those constituencies, serves neither the public nor private interest. The role of the director is to represent all the owners of the corporation and to consider the interests of all who have demands on it.

By responding to change in its external environment, business is changing in ways that are making it increasingly responsive to society's needs.

But, at the same time, it is resisting pressures to act in ways that would irreparably weaken its ability to fulfill its essential responsibility to the American people. It is not the *primary* role of business to clean up the environment, or decide what is best for consumers, or assure equal treatment for all—although it shares a responsibility to help attain these goals in the context of its own operations. The real role of business is the very unique one of creating or generating wealth— bringing together natural, capital and human resources in productive enterprise. And to the extent that business permits itself to be divorced from that prime responsibility, it ceases to be an asset to society and becomes a liability.

As we look to the future, it is imperative that the nation recognize the need to maintain and strengthen the primary role of business in *creating* wealth. The present preoccupation with *sharing* wealth is leading to a problem that Canadian industrialist V. O. Marquez has expressed this way:

> Governments, in their efforts to be responsive to the impractical idealists and to placate the power-seekers, are yielding to the growing pressures of the environmental electorate, and are constantly exploring or establishing new and

36

more difficult standards for the wealth-generating institutions to meet, and, thus, gradually reducing their ability to perform their primary and essential social function.[4]

In brief, business can and must be responsive to the changing needs of people—but it must be permitted to do so within the context of its basic role as a generator of wealth. For if it fails to fulfill this role, there will be little for society to share.

CHAPTER 4

————— ✳ —————

Business and Government

My first years with Sun Oil Company coincided with the flood of regulatory measures that were issuing from Congress and the Executive Branch in the early 1930s to deal with the problems of the Great Depression.

Those measures marked the start of a new era in business-government relations, and two of my first major assignments involved me very directly in it. The first was a survey of company operations relative to the requirements of the National Industrial Recovery Act. And the second was preparation of testimony for submission to the Temporary National Economic Committee, which, under Senator Joseph O'Mahoney, was investigating economic concentration in America.

In the intervening years, I have represented my company and the petroleum industry many times in testifying before Congressional committees and regulatory agencies. More recently, in the stormy years of the emerging energy crisis, I have devoted the major share of my time as Sun's chief executive officer to company and industry matters relating to government.

Over these past 40 years, I have directly observed a steady broadening of government regulation. Today the force of government is felt in virtually all major areas of business activity, including pricing decisions, employee compensation, hiring, product content, financial reporting, pollution control, advertising and customer relations. As regulation has broadened, the job of managing a business has become increasingly complex in terms of complying with specific rules, in providing an increasing volume of data to a growing number of government agencies and in presenting views and recommendations on mushrooming legislative and regulatory proposals. The cost of all this to business in time and talent has been heavy, indeed.

Comparing today's experiences with 40 years ago, however, I am increasingly impressed by this fact: There has been a discernible change in business-government relationships in the direction of increased understanding, cooperation and joint endeavor.

This is not to say that business and government now agree on all, or even most, issues. Or that business accepts as desirable or useful the complex regulation that now marks some areas of the economy. Or that progress toward more productive relations has been even and steady. The fact that there are still major problem areas is attested by the strained relationships that surround consideration of energy supply problems.

But business and government are forging new and closer relationships today that promise new strength for America tomorrow. I see two major forces behind this change. One is the growing complexity of the issues that society must deal with. It has been said that this is a time when great things must be done quickly, and surely the need for cleaning up the environment supports that view. Dealing effectively with such problems literally demands the cooperative efforts of government and business.

The second force flows from the rising expectations of the American people, expectations which reflect past economic and social progress in this country. People increasingly look to business *and* government together for the fulfillment of their expectations, and a growing perception of this shared responsibility is drawing the two institutions more closely together. Support for full employment and equal opportunity are cases in point.

The evolution of business-government relations to the present state has been marked by a continuing, if irregular, advance in government involvement in establishing the framework within which business operates. The pattern of relationships in earlier years generally reflected the American ideological concept of limited government, which is pretty well summed up in the phrase "the less government the better." Accordingly, there was little government regulation of the type known today until the late 1800s. In that period, passage of the Interstate Commerce Act (1887) and the Sherman Act (1890), following disputes over freight rates and some predatory business actions, reflected a public recognition that some form of regulation of competition was necessary. This was followed in the early years of the twentieth century by the Federal

Trade Commission Act and other measures designed to establish the guidelines for business competition.

The early 1930's brought a new wave of government regulation. Richard H. Holton of the University of California suggests that the public viewed the Depression as evidence that all was not necessarily going well in the economy following the 1920's version of a *laissez-faire* policy. A flood of new agencies to control business resulted, including the Securities and Exchange Commission, the Federal Communications Commission and the National Labor Relations Board.

Following World War II, passage of the Employment Act of 1946 moved government into implementing a set of policies designed to promote economic growth. Key tools used to accomplish this have been fiscal and monetary policies that stimulate investment and increase employment and income. While generally supporting these goals, many in business, myself included, continue to sharply question the deficit financing that frequently accompanies government efforts to accomplish them, and to urge that government policies recognize the vital need to control inflation.

Regulatory measures designed to control the performance of the market have been the principal focus of government-industry confrontations in the post World War II period, however. Business today generally supports the need for government to establish the ground rules to which all must adhere. But trouble develops when restrictions are imposed which clearly impair or inhibit the operation of market forces.

A striking example of this, relating to the petroleum industry, is federal control of field prices of natural gas. A 1954 Supreme Court decision held that gas production was subject to the Natural Gas Act of 1938, which was designed primarily to provide federal utility regulation of interstate gas pipelines and in which Congress had included a provision specifically exempting gas production and gathering. The fact is that America's more than 4,000 gas producers are clearly not public utilities in any sense of the concept. For they are not protected by government license from competition in any market and are not guaranteed any rate of return on investment, but instead compete against one another and against alternate fuels. Still, regulation and price control have continued for 20 years, with disastrous results for the domestic energy supply situation.

Regulation designed to protect the broad public interest in areas such as environmental conservation is relatively new, but highly significant for the future. It involves, typically, the establishing of standards by government, and the imposition of penalties when these are not met. The levels at which standards are to be set are the chief issues, and the focus of government-business interfaces in this area.

Against this background, several observations can be made about the nature of business-government relationships and the direction in which they have been evolving in recent years.

One is that business and government have traditionally been in an adversary relationship. Initially, the concept of limited government translated into business opposition to any broadening of government authority in economic matters. Accordingly, business generally has strongly opposed new regulatory measures that would interfere with or impair the operation of market forces.

This stance has frequently been interpreted as automatic opposition to government initiatives of any kind, and a quite negative public image of business has resulted. In fact, a businessman, S. J. Goodman, chairman of May Department Stores, has indicted business for its "almost unbroken record of opposing legislation that the public thinks is good."

This is seriously overstating the case, in my view; for there are few, if any, issues on which business speaks with one voice. But Mr. Goodman's comment does point up the positive role that business has played in restraining government.

In many ways, this role is a positive force for the nation, a needed restraint that the *Wall Street Journal* has described in these words:

> The business community has played a conservative role within the political framework, resisting change for the sake of change. But that is a crucial role that business leaders must play or it will not be played at all. Above all else, business seeks stability. Perhaps this is not the loftiest of goals. But it is not a trivial one, either. . . . There must be resistance to the myriad panaceas that are forever bubbling from the fertile minds of the nation's innovators and dreamers. And it can only be a business, attuned to reality, that is in a position to try to sift out only those that have at least a remote chance of doing more good than harm.[1]

One reason why business must play this role is the fact that its job is to *produce*—in the broad sense, wealth, and, in a narrower sense, individual goods and services. How well it meets this responsibility is the basis on which it is judged by society. So it must work to maintain the conditions and the climate under which it can produce to serve people.

While business has traditionally been associated with a defensive posture, it is true also that a new business role relative to government has been evolving. It is a role characterized not by "resistance" or "opposition," but by discussion, consultation, recommendation and response. This is not to say, of course, that business always, or even most of the time, agrees with government initiatives; but it is to say that in agreement or disagreement business increasingly is responsive.

I can identify three aspects of the new business approach that I feel are representative of change. And I will seek to illustrate these with examples from my own experience in the petroleum industry.

First, business is increasingly aware of its obligation to provide government with background information and recommendations on problems and issues. This is significant, because it is frequently the case that only business has the experience and know-how that is essential to informed government policy formulation and decision-making.

An outstanding example of this kind of business support is the series of energy studies prepared by the National Petroleum Council for government in recent years.

It was becoming apparent back in 1970 that the United States faced an energy supply problem of massive proportions. At that time, the Department of the Interior requested the National Petroleum Council, an official industry advisory board made up of representatives of large and small companies, to undertake a comprehensive study of the nation's energy outlook and to indicate where federal policies and programs could contribute to the achieving of long-term goals.

The Council responded by establishing committees and task forces utilizing the knowledge and skills of more than 200 representatives of the oil, gas, coal, nuclear and other energy industries, as well as a number of financial specialists. Over a period of some two years, these groups carried out detailed analyses of the U.S. energy situation, projected alternative supply situations and developed recommendations for government action.

The results of their research and study were published in a massive volume in December, 1972. Since that time, their work has served government and others as a basic resource and reference for dealing with a wide variety of energy-related problems and issues. I served as vice-chairman of the Council during the period of the study, and I can testify personally to the time and talent contributed to this effort by individual companies to provide a base for the development of national energy policies.

As the energy supply situation worsened, other industry groups and many individual companies have supported government by providing statistical and technical data essential to policy formulation, by consultation on specific problems and by furnishing recommendations for actions to strengthen domestic energy supply.

More broadly, a number of business-supported organizations have over a long period been focusing the experience and expertise of the private sector on the solution of public problems through continuing research and policy studies. Among these are the Brookings Institution, the Committee for Economic Development, the National Industrial Conference Board and the American Enterprise Institute for Public Policy Research.

Second, it is my observation that business is increasingly evaluating government proposals objectively and providing active support for those that promise to be helpful in better meeting the needs of the American people.

The energy field again provides an example. Specifically, the Administration has proposed the formation of a Department of Natural Resources, which would bring together in one unit all the energy-related functions of the federal government. Although this runs counter to the concept of decentralized government, it makes a great deal of practical sense in terms of coordinated administration of national energy policies. And the petroleum industry, including Sun Oil Company, is supporting the proposal.

Another example, of a completely different nature, is the support provided by business for the initial temporary program for controlling prices and wages as an anti-inflation measure in 1971. That support was provided in an effort to help government deal with a major national problem, although business was well aware of the market distortions that could—and, not surprisingly, unfortunately did—result.

Third, business has worked increasingly to provide policy and action alternatives to government in those areas where it feels government proposals are unnecessarily restrictive, or are likely to be ineffective or harmful to the functioning of the market.

One example of such activity in the energy area is the position taken by business in responding to environmental control measures. The petroleum industry was convinced from the beginning that the provisions of the 1970 Air Quality Act were unnecessarily exacting and that they would boost fuel consumption and lead to wasteful use of capital resources. Rather than simply oppose the standards, however, the petroleum industry developed a series of counter-proposals designed to achieve key environmental goals and, at the same time, to avoid unnecessary costs and regulation.

Sun Oil Company, for instance, recommended to government that automotive emission standards be held at existing levels until further research indicated what the appropriate future levels should be. At the same time, it was suggested that vehicle emission standards could be met more effectively through alternative engine designs that would not require expensive and potentially unreliable catalytic mufflers. And it was pointed out that overly strict emission standards could delay the development of alternative engine designs that would perform better for motorists and cost them less.

The petroleum industry has also taken the initiative in proposing to government those measures that its experience indicates are essential to strengthening domestic energy security, including the de-control of natural gas prices and accelerated leasing of federal energy lands. Further, it has backed up these recommendations with various types of informational programs designed to achieve the higher level of govern-

47

ment and public understanding required to secure action in these areas.

In brief, business is moving toward new and more productive relationships with government in ways that are increasing the responsiveness of both business and government to the American people.

Looking to the future, I suggest there will be an increasing need for joint action and harmonious relationships between business and government as economic and social issues become increasingly complex. But there may be some roadblocks ahead, too.

George Cabot Lodge of Harvard University has clearly articulated the potential problems we face, in pointing to the need for a renovation of U.S. ideology.

Our traditional ideology, he says, rests upon a number of principles that have come to us from European political thought of the seventeenth and eighteenth centuries. These are essentially that all men are born free and equal, that the origin and basis of government is the consent of the governed, that individual rights are of primary importance and that the least government is the best.

We tend to cling to that ideology today in thought and discussion, but in action we depart significantly from it. Our success in dealing with problems in America has largely been achieved through pragmatic approaches—approaches which center on finding workable solutions, and which reflect the belief that what works is good and true.

Therein lies the problem, a problem posed by change issues which are rooted in ideological contradictions. For example, infringements on the right of private property are ideologically undesirable; but,

48

practically, such infringements are precisely what are occurring in efforts to achieve the national goal of environmental improvement. Again, full employment is a desirable, practical goal; but achieving it runs counter to traditional ideology in regard to government planning for resource allocation and potential restrictions on the freedom of both individuals and enterprises.

Lodge reaches this conclusion:

> It is no longer realistic to suppose that the old ideology can remain part of the substratum of American life while pragmatic adjustments are made on the surface. The speed and profundity of change required are too great to allow for the short-term experimentation of the pragmatist; we need some new and more explicit framework to bring basic values to bear directly on the world around us.[2]

In these terms, the challenge we face is the most difficult one of bringing ideology and practice into conformity. And this has significant implications for both business and government.

One of the most significant is the issue of public versus private decision-making. Practice, it seems to me, has been leading increasingly toward public, or governmental, decision-making. While this is perhaps unavoidable in a limited number of areas, I think it is imperative that in re-defining ideology we retain a commitment to private decision-making.

Lee Loevinger, former assistant attorney general in charge of the Anti-Trust Division, has argued this point in an admirable manner. Contrasting the impacts of public and private decision-making, he makes this observation:

> Business decisions that are ill-informed, badly motivated or otherwise wrong may be ruinous to business and harmful to a number of people, but they are not ruinous to society. Government decisions that are ill-informed, badly motivated or wrong are not likely to be ruinous or even disadvantageous to those who make them, *but they can be ruinous to society.* Decisions by a government agency do not permit those who disagree to patronize a competitive government. Consequently, a decision by a government agency usually forecloses the possibility of learning the consequences of an alternative decision. Therefore, *wrong decisions by government agencies are often not even discovered to be wrong until conditions become intolerable.*[3]

American business and American government are engaged in the process of working out, slowly and unevenly, a new relationship and a new balance of power. In my view, this process promises to help us avoid that excessive concentration of power in government that would destroy the concept of private freedom and responsibility that is at the heart of the American experiment. It promises, too, to produce a new shared capability of business and government to deal more effectively with America's pressing economic and social problems.

Part II

---*---

BUSINESS AND SOCIETY

CHAPTER 5

———✱———

The Role of Profits in Serving Society

THE internal change that is making business more responsive to the needs of the American people has been paralleled externally by a sweeping advance in public expectations.

In broad perspective, the public is looking to business to assume new responsibilities, responsibilities reaching far beyond its traditional function of producing goods and services. The Committee for Economic Development has identified the thrust of this change in these words:

> The large business corporation is undergoing the most searching public scrutiny since the 1930s about its role in American society . . . it is clear that the terms of the contract between society and business are changing in substantial and important ways. Business is being asked to

assume broader responsibilities to society than
ever before, and to serve a broader range of
human values. Business enterprises in effect are
being asked to contribute more to the quality of
American life than just supplying quantities of
goods and services.[1]

This shifting perception of the role of business
demands careful examination since business exists to
serve society—and since the future of both ultimately depends upon how well business fulfills that
responsibility.

In this respect, the present state of affairs has dis-
quieting aspects. One of these is widespread ignorance
of how the private enterprise–profit business system
really works. This has spawned sharply critical public
views of some aspects of business performance, and
a latent hostility that threatens over time to seriously
weaken the ability of business to fill *any* useful role in
society. Much of the criticism stems from a lack of
understanding of the role of profits. This is central to
the entire issue of business responsibility, since the
profit concept relates not only to economic affairs but
also goes directly to the heart of the social system that
guarantees freedom.

The appalling lack of economic understanding in
this country is a national embarrassment, one shared
by all institutions, business, education and government alike. Consider the following.

Over a period of years, the profits earned by American business have averaged a 4 to 5 percent return on
sales after taxes. But the broadly held public view,
according to national opinion surveys, is that business
earns a return of approximately 28 percent. Astonish-

ingly, this gross misconception of business profitability exists broadly across society, among all kinds of people. Those in professional and managerial groups, for example, estimate the average return on sales at 26 percent, while those generally considered to be "thought leaders" say the average return is 27 percent.

Further, more than one-third of the public—35 percent—say business makes too much profit and 40 percent feel that government should limit the profits of business. Most people appear to believe that the system doesn't share fairly, since two in three say companies make so much profit that they could afford to raise wages without raising prices. And half of the public expresses the general view that the profits of large companies do not contribute to making things better.

Views such as these are increasingly engendering feelings of mistrust, suspicion and open hostility that threaten to cripple the capabilities of business and the business system.

Against this background, it is essential that business reappraise its relationships with the American people, seeking new approaches to achieving an improved understanding of the nature of the business system and its importance to gaining national goals. Basic to this is improved public understanding of the role of profits in our society.

While the concept of the profit system is a fairly simple one, it has been obfuscated by rhetoric and finely shaded theoretical argument. Cutting through the verbiage to the heart of the matter, the functions of profits shape up like this:

Profits are the *inducement* to investors to risk savings in the face of uncertainty. They are the *reward* to investors for success. They are the *yardstick* for measuring the performance of those who manage the capital invested in business. They are the *means* of allocating resources among businesses; for example, when rising, they attract capital for needed expansion. They are the primary *source* of venture capital for modernization, expansion and the creation of new enterprises.

In other words, profits are the driving force in the economy, the force that provides and attracts capital for job-creating and wealth-producing investment in new and expanded enterprises.

In performing these functions, profits make a broad contribution to economic and social progress, a contribution that John Diebold, broadly experienced management scientist and executive, has expressed in these words:

> I believe that profit-seeking enterprise—despite its many faults—does provide the best mechanism we have for spurring efficiency in resource allocation, for encouraging innovation and application of resources in entirely new modes, for securing the transference of resources to new product lines or to play an entirely different role in society. Also, private businesses have the great advantage that they can and do disappear when they are not doing a relevant and effective job any longer.[2]

The profit dollars that are required to perform these functions add up to a relatively small part of the wealth produced in America, although this is little understood by most Americans. But the fact is that the combined profits of all enterprises in the nation amount to less than 10 percent of national income.

Small though it may be, this profits segment of the nation's income is the lifeblood of the economy. The experience of the petroleum industry in recent years demonstrates why this is so, and why regulation that impinges on profitability can have a disastrous impact on essential economic activity.

Due principally to direct and indirect price controls on natural gas and oil, petroleum industry profits were severely depressed during the five-year period ending in 1972. Reflecting this, return on stockholders' equity fell from 12.9 percent in 1968 to 10.8 percent in 1972. The industry's ability to generate capital for investment through profits was substantially weakened, and it was forced to turn increasingly to external financing. At the close of 1972, the long-term debt of a group of 30 large, integrated firms was equivalent to more than 30 percent of invested capital, up from 15 percent just 10 years earlier—and coming very close to the level that is considered to be a practical limit for a high-risk activity such as petroleum development.

This weakening of the industry's profit position, particularly in relation to U.S. operations, was reflected in a substantial decline in domestic petroleum exploration and development efforts. Drilling fell off drastically, the earlier thrust of domestic investment was blunted and petroleum reserves began to decline not only relatively in relation to demand, but absolutely. And these trends were at the heart of the energy crisis that hit the United States full-force in 1973.

The severe petroleum shortages that developed then led to price increases, even under continuing controls, and profits improved substantially during the year. The impact on domestic petroleum exploration was almost immediate.

By the close of 1973, the number of drilling rigs in operation was up 15 percent from the comparable period a year earlier. Natural gas discoveries were on the rise. Investment in domestic petroleum exploration and development and in related facilities began to climb sharply, following a period of stagnation. A group of large, integrated companies hiked planned U.S. capital outlays by 50 percent in 1974 to more than $8.5 billion.

In other words, profits were doing their job of providing and attracting investment capital, and thereby launching the long, hard climb back to a prudent level of domestic energy self-sufficiency for the United States.

To carry this illustration one step further, the improvement in petroleum profits during 1973 met with considerable hostility on the part of government and the public. The petroleum industry was widely criticized for making unconscionable earnings at the expense of the American public in a shortage situation. And a variety of proposals were brought forth to tax away "windfall" petroleum profits.

The fact is, of course, that improved profits were precisely what was needed to spark increased energy development. But the public's failure to understand this threatened—and continues to threaten—the industry's ability to generate the needed investment dollars.

Writing in the *Wall Street Journal*, W. Philip Graham and Richard H. Davis of Texas A. & M. appraised the situation this way:

> Under a free enterprise system the only way that the cash flow and incentives necessary for research and exploration can be provided is from profits. . . . Somewhere along the line people have forgotten how the profit system works, that it is to each producer's self-interest to expand output and thereby expand profits. As each producer does this, excess profits are competed away. Excess profits vanish when their work is done and output has increased.[3]

It is increasingly apparent that continuation of this low level of economic understanding poses very grave problems for America. The nation is operating at high levels of economic and political risk today. And it simply cannot afford the growing divisiveness that strikes at the heart of its ability to move society in the direction that people want it to go.

Accordingly, all American institutions are challenged today to find new approaches to gaining a higher level of public awareness and understanding of economic principles. Looking at this challenge from the business viewpoint, my experience suggests that, in responding, consideration should be given to the following matters.

One is the need to clearly articulate the purpose of the business system. I think that we in business have erred grievously in the past in projecting the notion that the *single purpose* of business is to make a profit. While it is doubtful that many businessmen really believe that, much of what is said comes out sounding as if they did.

Business needs to clearly project its commitment to the purpose of satisfying the needs of people—in the narrow sense, the needs of today's customers, and, in a broader sense, the needs of society. And it must make clear that earning a profit is essential to fulfilling that purpose.

Business must also demonstrate a full commitment to the private enterprise system.

Basic tenets of the system are acceptance of risk, a commitment to compete vigorously and a willingness to stand or fall on the basis of performance in a free market. When enterprises do not honor these tenets, the system does not function properly. And when this occurs, public confusion about its purpose and performance is understandable.

Most frequently, such problems arise when a business seeks protection from competition through government intervention. One government official has referred to "numerous instances in which business turned to government to seek forms of assistance which, in effect, would reduce competition—for example, asking for imposition of subsidies or tariffs, occupational licensing, fair trade laws and import quotas."

To cite one example, the petroleum industry in the past was severely criticized for supporting government limitation of the volume of foreign oil imported. The fact was that import controls were deemed necessary by government on the grounds of national security, and properly so. But it is also true that the nature of the control program created distortions in the market and led to considerable public confusion and hostility. In retrospect, a control system more closely aligned with free market principles would have better served the interests of all.

Another major consideration for business is a re-orientation of its communications about profit and performance.

The increasingly competitive struggle for capital has tended to lead business into the trap of orienting much of its communication to the interests of the financial community and large investors. The tendency of business schools to stress the bottom line in management training has reinforced this trend. And the result is a heavy communication emphasis on increases in dollar earnings and on earnings per share of stock.

Two kinds of problems have resulted. One is that much financial communication assumes a sophisticated knowledge that most readers don't really have. And the other is that a myopic focus on what are sometimes miniscule earnings gains has created strong misimpressions about the level and adequacy of profits.

Max Ways has pointed out in *Fortune* that substantial percentage increases in reported profits can mask returns on sales and investment that are meager or barely adequate. And he goes on to say:

> When headlines say "QED Corporation's Profits Up 33%," a lot of people get a mistaken impression of what has happened, and George Meany will find a resounding public echo when he speaks of the "unconscionable profits" received by corporations.[4]

The solution to this difficulty, of course, is not to provide less information to the investment community, but to provide more information to others—information that is relevant to the interests and knowledge of the general public and that is provided in the context of overall performance rather than just earnings performance.

There are broad opportunities to do so. For example, much more emphasis can be placed on how profits are used. This is particularly true in relation to demonstrating that profits go into the new facilities and equipment that enable companies to strengthen their competitive positions, create new jobs, increase the security of existing jobs and expand the output of products that people need. At Sun Oil Company, we have stressed the fact that profits fall far short of investment needs—that for every dollar earned in profits we are investing two to three dollars in the development of new supplies of energy and in related facilities.

My experience suggests also that business generally must become more open in communication. It has been said that in many companies no piece of information is ever released if one department can think of a single reason for not doing so. And business journalists cite horrible examples of corporate non-communication, evasion and legal filtering that are not at all uncommon.

Resolving this issue can present real problems, however, since business obviously cannot operate in a goldfish bowl. But neither can it erect barriers to releasing information except that judged to be safe and favorable to the corporation; for public trust and confidence are unlikely to result from such a policy. The answer lies in a balanced release of information that safeguards proprietary data but also reflects a commitment to keeping investors and the public fully and frankly informed about the company's performance and prospects.

Beyond the business community, government and the educational system also carry heavy responsibilities for helping to achieve improved public understanding of the business system.

Government, for example, must assure the freedom from unnecessary regulation that is essential to the system's responding effectively to the changing needs of people. This requires that government refrain from politically popular but economically disastrous sallies into experimental regulation that stifle market forces. The imposition of price and wage controls in the early 1970s is a precise example of what should be avoided. These not only badly distorted markets, but at the same time led to increased hostility toward business since profit increases in a controlled economy were viewed with suspicion.

Over and above its traditional responsibilities, the educational system has a particularly important role to play in achieving economic understanding. The political structure of this country requires that individuals make decisions about issues, some of the most important of which are economic in nature. Today many, if not most, people are not prepared to do so. For their level of economic understanding is simply not up to that required for intelligent decision-making. We must look to the educational system at all levels, with business and government support, to prepare all Americans to participate effectively in this decision-making process.

There are two other overriding considerations to which all of us must give thoughtful attention if we are really to reach that state of understanding and support that will enable our economic system to serve us fully.

One problem is that we are demanding more from our business system at the same time that we are limiting its ability to deliver. A refrain of contradictory demands is being heard around the country today, but we seem to be unable even to perceive that they are in conflict with each other.

C. Jackson Grayson, reflecting on his experience as chairman of the Price Commission, has described the situation in these words:

> I heard demands for increased pollution controls but, at the same time, for lower transportation prices, increased health benefits but lower hospital costs, increased mine safety but lower coal prices, decreased insecticide usage but lower food prices, protected forests but lower lumber prices. . . .[5]

It is apparent that we need to sort out our priorities on what it is that we want, at the same time realizing that increased productivity is the key to real improvement in our economic and social situation.

A second problem, also recognized by Mr. Grayson, is that a growing effort to insulate the nation from the impact of economic change is inhibiting the functioning of our business system. My own concern is that to the extent we move away from the concepts of risk and competition we also weaken incentives to excel.

The dilemma is that without such incentives our system simply will not work. It is essential that we unleash our private enterprise–profit system and permit it to function as designed in helping us to achieve the rising level of expectations in our society.

CHAPTER 6

———•✳•———

Appraising Corporate Social Responsibility

> The sharp rise in public expectations for business in a wide assortment of areas hitherto regarded as public responsibilities is one of the most significant developments in modern American public opinion.[1]

THIS was the Harris Survey's appraisal in the early 1970s of the growing public desire for business to provide leadership in dealing with major national social problems. Specific probing of public attitudes revealed that upwards of 5 of every 10 Americans felt that business should take the lead in dealing with such widely diverse problems as preserving the environment, wiping out poverty and raising moral standards.

These emerging public desires have sparked a wide-ranging debate involving virtually all the nation's institutions over the past 10 years. The debate focuses on the social responsibilities of the corporation. And it seeks to define a new role for American business—over and above its traditional task of supplying goods and services—in regard to the nature and extent of its involvement in the solution of critical social problems.

The issues under discussion have important implications not only for business but for all other segments of American society. For they involve, basically, a rewriting of the social contract governing relationships among and between individuals and institutions. Already it is clear that substantial changes in those relationships are occurring, and that they are impacting significantly on the management of American business. One result is severe criticism of business by some for its "slow, cautious and wholly inadequate" response to social change.

At this stage of the debate, three general observations can be made.

One, there is broad agreement that the *primary* role of business is the economic one of producing the goods and services society needs.

Two, there is broad *disagreement* about what the additional "social" role of business is, if, indeed, there is any.

Three, there are initial indications that a common view is gradually evolving, and that it embraces an enlarged social concern on the part of business. Writing in the *Columbia Journal of World Business*, Melvin Anshen has pointed out that there is an emerging shift in the conceptual relationships between economic growth and social progress. In the past, he said, the primacy of economic growth relative to social considerations went unchallenged. Today it is widely challenged; and in the future, he predicts, social considerations—or, broadly, the quality of life —will weigh equally with economic considerations in business decision-making.

There is by no means a consensus on this point of view, however. In fact, at the risk of oversimplification, three basic positions on corporate responsibility can be identified.

At the one extreme are those who hold that the "business of business is business." Perhaps the most eloquent spokesman for this view is Milton Friedman, who states the position this way in his book *Capitalism and Freedom:*

> There is one and only one social responsibility of business—to use its resources and engage in activities designed to increase its profits so long as it stays within the rules of the game, which is to say, engages in open and free competition, without deception or fraud.[2]

At the other extreme are those who hold that corporations are primarily to blame for the nation's economic and social ills and, therefore, are directly responsible for solving the problems we face. This view holds, in effect, that the rules of the game have changed and that business will play under the new rules or not at all.

Positioned at various points across the broad middle are most businessmen and many of their critics. Characterizing this diverse group is a general agreement that business must respond in new ways to the changing social environment, but that this response should be within the basic context of the private enterprise system. The Committee for Economic Development has described this position as "enlightened self-interest" which aims to "release the full productive and organizational capacities of the corporation for the benefit of society."

It is this middle view, I feel, that positions business correctly in relation to new responsibilities. Mr. Friedman's stance is certainly valid in the sense that earning a profit is essential to survival. But I feel that earning a profit in itself is not enough, in view of the sweeping change in our society and the complexity in public problems that has resulted. On the other hand, the assertion that the rules of the game have changed, and that the social role now over-rides the economic, goes too far. For whatever social contribution business can make must be made from the base of its economic strength.

There are probably as many personal views of business corporate responsibility as there are businessmen. My own view, reflecting the stance of Sun Oil Company, is this:

I feel that the basic role of business in society is to provide, reliably and profitably, those goods and services that the public most fundamentally expects it—or depends upon it—to supply. For if we cannot be counted upon for this, then surely we cannot be counted upon for much of anything else that is helpful to our society.

Providing what the public wants, and doing so *reliably*, means several things:

> ... It means planning ahead, such as for future supply; individuals tend to be pretty happy-go-

lucky about the future, but a responsible business cannot be so.

... It means managing resources with an eye to continuity, even when tomorrow's needs require sacrificing today's advantage.

... It means speaking out on policies that will affect our ability to deliver in the future, even when such speaking out is unpopular.

... It means dealing honorably—behaving reliably, exercising integrity, avoiding guile.

Providing what the public wants, and doing so *profitably*, means several other things:

... It means maximizing resource utilization —using resources as efficiently as possible—for this is the basis of all of man's advancement in material welfare.

... It means generating the capital which is basic to continued production, and without which planning is merely an empty exercise.

... It means being innovative—in resource use and technology—for innovation is the cutting edge of qualitative growth.

... Finally, it means actually earning a profit in the marketplace—a return competitive with that from similar investments and sufficient to generate and attract the capital required for renewal and growth.

Providing what people look to business for, and doing so both reliably and profitably, is at the heart of discharging responsibility to the public. It is neither a narrow concept, nor a superficial view of social responsibility. Nor does it encompass all that is acceptable as a proper definition of that responsibility. But it is the bedrock to which extensions of the role of business must be anchored.

Peter Drucker said it well, I think, when he argued that organizations are socially responsible "when they satisfy society's needs through concentration on their own specific jobs."

In defining this role, I am not suggesting that business has completely fulfilled it. Obviously, it has not. In the case of the petroleum industry, for example, current energy scarcity points to the need for a broader approach to long-range planning for future supply and resource continuity. Fewer than 10 years ago, virtually the entire industry was supporting a "discover America by car" campaign to promote increased automobile travel. This was part of an industry-wide scramble to maintain position in the face of profit pressures by selling the incremental barrel. It was a struggle to avoid losing ground to the detriment of stockholders and employees, and it attests to the fiercely competitive nature of the business. In retrospect, however, what was an understandable short-term strategy becomes questionable in the face of impending energy scarcity in the longer term. It is clear, today, I think, that in the future our business and others must evaluate alternative courses of action more carefully in terms of the public interest.

Once this *basic* role has been established, it is possible to then consider in what ways business can broaden its service to society. This can build naturally upon the past; for business has over a period of many years, while carrying out its economic role, made social contributions, too. Corporate gifts to charitable and community service organizations are perhaps the leading example of such contributions. Another is corporate support for educational institutions. Another is the varied support given to local community organizations and activities in areas where major corporate facilities are located.

From this earlier base of social involvement, there has been a substantial broadening of corporate activity in the past decade. Reflecting this, business is engaged today in such varied activities as providing financial support and technical assistance for minority enterprises, furnishing special vocational training and career counseling for the disadvantaged, engaging in urban renewal and development, providing financial support for culture and the arts, supporting resource conservation and preservation, and working for improved medical and health care.

While the sum of these efforts is small in the total picture of social needs, such activities reflect an evolving, growing role for business in contributing to improving the quality of life. At the same time, it is important to recognize that the defining of this new role is still in its infancy and that hard questions must be faced in the years ahead in balancing desired social improvement in the near-term with preserving the vitality and capability of the economic system in the longer-term.

The central issue for the future is how and under what conditions business will seek to, and be permitted to, fulfill an expanding social role.

There are two ways our nation could go here. One involves the increasing application of public pressure that could force, or possibly lead, business into social responses that would gain short-run objectives at the price of literally destroying the capability for longer-run progress. This, I think, is one of the concerns of Mr. Friedman when he talks about businessmen being "unwitting puppets of the intellectual forces that have been undermining the basis of a free society." And I would agree that the potential for this exists in the shaping of a new role for business.

The challenge to business, and to society, is to successfully travel the other route of voluntary, cooperative response. This charges business, first, with fully perceiving a new role and, second, with developing out of its rich resources of human talent and technological thrust fresh and creative private sector approaches to public problems.

At the same time, this approach imposes upon society the responsibility for providing the freedom of action—the free play of market incentives and forces and individual responses to them—that is the essential prerequisite for innovation and progress.

I am not suggesting that the "invisible hand" will automatically assure maximum performance in the public interest as individual enterprises strive to obtain their individual goals. For this is not necessarily true in relation to discerning and serving the public interest on complex present-day issues that involve interrelated economic and social considerations. But I am suggesting that we heed the warning that Adam Smith appended to his thought about the merchant who, in following his own self interest, promoted "an end which was not part of his intention." Smith added:

Nor is it always the worse for the society that it was no part of it. By pursuing his own interest he frequently promotes that of the society more effectually than when he really intends to promote it. I have never known much good done by those who have affected to trade for the public good.[3]

In other words, the accumulated thrust of private endeavor is usually the most effective means of advancing the public interest. And we need to be aware of that in shaping our efforts to deal with the social problems of the day.

This means, too, that business must discipline its responses to social challenges, for it will make the greatest and most lasting contributions when it seeks to act on specific problems in the areas of its own experience and expertise. Voltaire said "let us cultivate our garden," and I think this is precisely the philosophy that will prove to be most productive in meeting social needs.

Several examples will demonstrate how Sun Oil Company is seeking to implement this philosophy; the activities cited are neither new nor unique, but they illustrate the point of working toward social goals in the context of our own business operations and experience.

In 1970, Sun implemented a minority vendor purchasing program specifically designed to support and strengthen small minority businesses by providing them opportunities to sell to us. Our approach was, and is, to search out vendors who show a reasonable potential for becoming competitive and to direct some of our business to them in a way that is not harmful to the position of our regular suppliers. Additionally, we are providing technical assistance and guidance to these vendors in financial, tax, legal and operating areas. The object is to help solve operational and managerial problems, and so sharpen the competence and competitive capabilities of minority companies.

In a similar fashion, we established and support a minority enterprise small business investment company (MESBIC). Through this we are providing management expertise, and assistance in the provision of capital, for small minority firms. The thrust of this effort, again, is to make the managerial and technical resources of the company available to help minority firms develop into viable businesses able to stand on their own feet in competitive markets.

Other related activities include company-wide banking programs for deposit of funds in minority banks located in our operating territory; training of unskilled and disadvantaged people in service station operation and management; assisting members of minority groups in financing their entry into the service station business; expanded financial support for minority schools and students; pre-employment training programs for those lacking formal education; and high-school tutorial and career-counseling programs.

These are small beginnings. They amount to not much more than providing equal opportunity. And we have encountered failures as well as successes. But they are beginnings—and beginnings that promise to have a long-run multiplier effect. What we are learning from our initial efforts should help us to work more effectively in these areas in the future.

In broader perspective, much more attention must be given to harnessing our private enterprise system to the fulfilling of social needs. It has been said that private affluence exists side-by-side with public squalor because business has focused its attention on producing those things that can be sold at a profit. This is true, of course, because only in this way can business survive. What is required, then, is not an effort to force business to engage in unprofitable activities, but an effort to direct the productive thrust of private business into areas of public need by making such activity profitable.

At the same time, increasing cooperation between the public and the private sectors will be required in the future. Business will bring to this alliance its diverse management capabilities, its proven ability to produce and the *discipline* of the profit system. Government's role will be to provide leadership in setting goals, establishing priorities and creating the conditions, including tax and other incentives, that are essential to harnessing the resources and capabilities of private business to the provision of services that are essential to improving the quality of living.

By linking the political and financial strength of government with the entrepreneurial thrust of business, maximum effectiveness can be gained in dealing with critical problems. This linkage may also require in some instances the development of new forms of public-private cooperation to deal with major social needs that cannot be met with more conventional approaches.

Underlying all of these observations about meeting social needs is the requirement that business commit itself to full involvement as a participant in the change that is occurring, rather than assuming the role of interested observer. Sociologist Daniel Yankelovich has suggested that business made a number of incorrect judgments on the basis of its early experience in the social responsibility area. Among these were the labeling of such activities as marginal relative to the ongoing business and optional in respect to how much or how little business should do. Not so, according to Mr. Yankelovich, who goes on to say:

> The claims of the public sector . . . have everything to do with the day-to-day operations of any company . . . above all, the decision of whether or not to heed the demands of the public sector is becoming less optional all of the time. The demands of the public sector are rapidly becoming translated into binding legislation by government, a precondition for winning the goodwill of the public, and an investment consideration by some institutional investors.[4]

It is a reasonable expectation that government will be increasingly involved in the meeting of public demands in the future and that the potential for "binding legislation" will increase. This prospect literally demands that business become directly and positively involved in the re-writing of the social contract. Failure to do so, as Melvin Anshen has pointed out, could leave the new rules to be formulated by "either the small group of critics armed only with malevolence toward the existing system, or the much larger group sincerely motivated by concern for ameliorating social ills but grossly handicapped by their ignorance of the techniques and dynamism of private enterprise."

76

In looking ahead to the further evolution of corporate social responsibility, I am reminded of the comment that what we need to do with the future is not to forecast it but to create it. Accordingly, the future that I see being created is this:

One, the business community will continue moving, somewhat unevenly, toward a new balance in its responsibilities—a balance that will necessarily lead to a new and deeper involvement in social issues and problems.

Two, our country will avoid imposing crippling political constraints on freedom of economic action and thereby avert patterns of response that would be counter-productive to both economic and social progress in the future.

Three, the broadened responsibility for business will evolve within the framework of the private enterprise system. But that result will not be won easily, nor by business alone. It will be won by all of us through a heightened perception of our common interests and how they can best be furthered and by our willingness to sacrifice superficial short-run gain for basic long-term progress.

In achieving this, we will be shaping out of a variety of possible futures one that reflects and supports the primacy of human values and the well-being of people.

CHAPTER 7

———— * ————

Must We Become a "Stationary" Society?

UNTIL a few years ago, economic growth was widely accepted as the key to continuing progress and an improving quality of life for people throughout the world. It would solve social problems. It would increase the incomes of the poor and the disadvantaged. It would lift the developing nations toward the affluence of their industrial neighbors. Finally, it would generally advance the world toward political, economic and social equilibrium.

Today, in the eyes of many, that view of growth is no longer valid. For them, the beneficent genie has become a villain. Increasingly, they are questioning not only the practical possibility of continuing growth, but also its value and desirability. Some are baldly asserting that growth is harmful and must be halted.

Must We Become a "Stationary" Society?

The idea is not a new one. Forty years ago, President Franklin D. Roosevelt described ours as a "mature economy." Long before that, John Stuart Mill pondered the concept of a stationary society in the nineteenth century, asking "when the (industrial) progress ceases, in what condition are we to expect that it will leave mankind?" But the notion of zero economic growth got scant attention during the industrial explosion of the past 100 years. Only recently has it become a subject of serious national debate and an issue of significance for American business management.

The concept owes much of its present notoriety to a scholarly looking little book produced in 1972 for the Club of Rome by a group of systems analysts at Massachusetts Institute of Technology. Entitled *The Limits to Growth*, its message is deceptively simple and shockingly blunt: *"Our civilization must limit growth or collapse."*

Ironically, this message that growth must end was delivered at the apex of an economic advance that was just beginning to make possible a broad effort to deal with nagging social problems. The *London Economist* had pointed out that in the United States "man's long economic problem is ending," at the same time warning that "his social problems still gape." In that situation, the warning that the economic advance upon which social progress depended could no longer be sustained served only to intensify already-severe internal tensions.

The questions raised in this debate over growth have impacted very directly on American business management. Much that is criticized about growth, including environmental pollution, is laid directly at the door of business or the ideology of the American business system. For this reason, and the additional reason that the growth controversy provides some insights into changing values in the United States today, the issue merits thoughtful examination and consideration from the business perspective.

The MIT researchers in *The Limits to Growth* hold basically that exponential growth is exhausting finite resources, and that continuation of present trends will lead to industrial collapse within the next century. Dennis Meadows, who headed the study team, flatly predicts that within the next few decades "there will likely be a marked decline in standards of living" and that "the world's population may experience a 'die-back' to more supportable levels, as a consequence of starvation, pollution and other factors."

In calling for limitations on growth now, while this is still possible, the study goes on to say:

> Man possesses for a small moment in his history, the most powerful combination of knowledge, tools and resources the world has ever known. He has all that is physically necessary to create a totally new form of human society— one that would be built to last for generations. The two missing ingredients are a realistic long-term goal that can guide mankind to the equilibrium society and the human will to achieve that goal.[1]

Another body of opinion is strongly anti-growth for reasons completely apart from the scarcity of resources. Probably its leading spokesman is E. J. Mishan, the British economist who has been called the "apostle of anti-growth."

Mr. Mishan holds that increasing affluence is more harmful than helpful to people. In countries such as the United States, he adds, growth is largely futile because economic status has become relative; and over time everybody cannot become relatively better off. In any case, he continues, "the more we produce our so-called amenities, such as automobiles, jet liners, television sets and electric drink stirrers, the more we also produce the disamenities like air and water pollution, traffic congestion, uninhabitable cities and massive dissatisfaction among the people."

Not the least of his concerns is the human dissatisfaction, which he ascribes to a decline in relationships among people as society becomes more affluent. He expresses his apprehension, movingly, in these words:

> It is sobering to wonder seriously if more and more of what is innately trivial is being gained at a cost of more and more that is innately valuable. Allow that the machine is incomparably efficient, can its efficiency in yielding services compensate for the inevitable loss of authentic human experience? Can anyone reasonably expect technological innovations in the future to be more humanizing?[2]

On the other side of the issue, it is argued that continuing economic growth is essential to human progress. My own observations of economic forces and human needs, and my professional experience in business, convince me that this is true.

In saying that, I am mindful of one observer's comment that only a madman or an economist is capable of believing that exponential growth could continue indefinitely in a world with finite resources. And my support for the growth concept is not a commitment to maximum physical production, but to a maximum effort to meet, *qualitatively* as well as quantitatively, the economic and social needs of people.

I am not insensitive to the finite nature of our resources. Nor am I unaware that some aspects of growth are negative. Nor am I opting for a wasteful use of resources in the disorganized pursuit of growth simply for its own sake. But I am opposed to the notion that people must be denied the benefits of economic progress now because there are risks and uncertainties in the future. We have always faced risk and uncertainty. And before we foreclose the future on those grounds, we ought to consider much more carefully than we already have the likely nature of a stationary society.

A distinguished group of contributors to the journal *Daedalus* examined this and other aspects of the no-growth concept in 1973, raising questions and proposing actions that deserve broad national consideration.

Right at the outset, they noted considerable disagreement about precisely what is meant by zero economic growth. In its most basic terms, a no-growth society would be one in which people could have no more of anything—even a cleaner environment—without giving up something they already have. But many who oppose growth do not seem to really want that. Rather, they envision a kind of selective growth, with limits on producing what they consider undesirable or unnecessary and expanded output of goods or services they see as useful and needed.

In any case, as Mancur Olson of the University of Maryland points out, a limited-growth society would be marked by very sharp conflicts over distribution. For, with stabilized output, one group could improve its position only at the expense of some other group.

In this respect, it is significant that even in the past two or three decades of real economic growth many people feel that they have not shared fairly in progress —that their gains are too little and achieved too slowly. In a stationary society, prospects for further gains through growth would be wiped out, and the only remaining avenue for bettering the position of low-income groups would be a massive re-distribution of income. That points very clearly to a potential confrontation between the poor and those who want to limit growth.

The no-growth concept has been likened in this regard to the affluent kicking down behind them the ladder on which they climbed to the top. And this raises obvious questions of equity and morality.

These considerations apply not only to individuals and to groups, but to nations. Even if it were assumed that industrial nations such as our own could accept the no-growth notion with some degree of equanimity, this is surely not true of the many developing nations around the globe. Those now arguing for limits on growth might profitably consider the question as to how these countries, straining on every front possible for an acceleration of economic growth, could be suddenly persuaded to give up this effort—and give it up permanently.

A preview of the reactions that would likely be encountered was provided by the United Nations Conference on the Environment in 1973. According to reports of that Conference, developing nations charged that limiting economic activity to gain environmental improvement was simply one more form of imperialism perpetrated by the industrial nations. And they made it very clear that they fully intended to go right on growing, pollution or no. It is likely that other arguments for limiting growth would be equally persuasive.

It is probable, also, that a stationary society would develop a psychology quite different from that which has marked the United States in the past. Mr. Olson makes this point:

> . . . there would be few, if any, frontiers or safety valves in a no-growth society. Where then should the discontented and the aggressive and the venturesome go? There would be few, if any, places for them to go, and so it seems not unreasonable to assume that a culture or consciousness would and should emerge which would minimize the number of people with dynamic and creative personality characteristics.[3]

Perhaps the most significant aspect of a no-growth society, however, would be the increased power and influence of government. Such a society would necessarily be marked by a very high degree of central regulation to impose the necessary constraints and to assure that growth was, indeed, halted. Also, with profit and price mechanisms no longer effectively governing the allocation of resources and effort, government would in some way have to plan this. Regulation would breed more regulation, and over time the traditional freedoms of Americans and American institutions would be gradually eroded.

Must We Become a "Stationary" Society?

Shrinking opportunity and increasing restraint are the antithesis of the conditions that have characterized the American experiment in the past. And it is highly unlikely that the thrust of its social advance could be sustained in a limited growth environment. The stationary state equates with loss of confidence in the future—and the impact of lessened confidence reaches far beyond the economic sphere into the roots of human values and aspirations.

The more closely the growth issue is examined in these terms, it seems to me the more clearly is it evident that growth is not the real issue. The real issue is how to most effectively meet human needs or, in other words, to advance the human condition. If it is agreed that this is the matter of primary concern, growth then can be viewed in a different perspective. For the focus then becomes how best to advance the human condition, rather than how best to adapt to limited resources or to accommodate ideological differences. In this perspective, limiting growth is akin to burning down the house to cook the breakfast. There are obviously more efficient and less destructive ways to do that, just as there are more efficient and less destructive ways than limiting growth to advance the human condition.

The starting point in shaping a new approach to growth is recognition of its essentiality to meeting human needs. I am not suggesting that the United States necessarily needs more automobiles or more color television sets. But it assuredly needs to improve the economic situation of millions of individual people, in terms of meeting such basic requirements as nutritious food and decent housing. It needs also to provide productive employment to millions of people who are now denied such opportunity. And it needs to better control pollution, to broaden educational opportunities and to improve health care. It can do none of these things effectively with zero economic growth.

If growth in this sense is positive, then the real question becomes how best to achieve its benefits while minimizing its harmful effects. I suggest the answer lies not in halting growth because some resources are limited, but in maintaining the economic freedom and incentive that will encourage the development of new resources in accordance with the needs of the people of the world. It is not unreasonable to expect that new resources and materials will be developed. After all, the world gets most of its energy today from a resource—petroleum—that was virtually unknown and unused just a little more than 100 years ago. How this came about is relevant to prospects for future growth.

Back in the 1800s, whale oil was widely used for lighting. As demand grew steadily, prices rose sharply. And the argument might well have been advanced in 1850 that use of the oil should be restricted since the supply of whales was obviously limited. What really happened, however, was that rising prices encouraged the development of petroleum as a new energy source. And petroleum, within a relatively short time, became the lifeblood of industrial enterprise.

Today supplies of petroleum are running short relative to demand, and prices are rising. Again, it could be argued that energy consumption, and the economic growth it fuels, should be tightly controlled because petroleum resources are finite and can be exhausted.

But what is really happening is that rising prices are encouraging the production of liquid fuels from coal and oil shale, and the initiation of efforts to develop other forms of energy. And further off on the horizon are energy from nuclear fusion and from the sun itself.

The daring, the vision and the creativity of people, linked with the thrust of technology, have accomplished much in the past. And it is a narrowly restrictive view of the future that assumes they cannot and will not accomplish much more.

The reforming of growth to meet qualitative standards is by no means impossible, either. Henry Wallich of Yale has advanced the suggestion that an effective way to accomplish this is through an extended version of the price system. For example, any harmful aspects of growth could be reflected fully in the costs of production and subsequently in the price to the consumer. This internalization of "externalities"—pollution and other costs of growth—would transfer the cost from the general public to the producers and consumers of the specific product involved in the pollution.

There are various other mechanisms for controlling the harmful effects of growth. One is regulation which stipulates what is acceptable performance. Another is the provision of tax incentives or subsidies. Refining approaches or techniques to achieve the most effective results in specific situations will not be easy. But, as Marc Roberts of Harvard has pointed out, "if the success even of subtle techniques is problematical, consider the pointlessness of trying to accomplish our aims by simply limiting economic growth."

There remains the ideological consideration that continuing economic growth is bad because it is dehumanizing—that it is harmful to individual human experience and that it lessens the quality of life.

In response to this view, I suggest that it has by no means been demonstrated that growth is *automatically* hurtful to the human condition.

I have observed the quality of life in some of the less developed countries, countries that have experienced far less economic growth than has the United States and are therefore necessarily considerably less materialistic. And it is my observation that the absence of economic growth can be dehumanizing, too—excruciatingly so. It is certainly true that most people in these nations live closer to the land and have more opportunities to enjoy its natural beauty. But I am not at all sure that in their poverty and need they consider this an advantage.

The thesis that affluence and the material gains that accompany it are harmful to human relationships is more difficult and complex. In some respects, I think the thesis is valid; long periods of intensive television viewing to the exclusion of other activities surely precludes positive interactions among family members, for example. But in other ways the reverse is true; for a family vacation, made possible by the automobile, encompassing some of the natural beauties of America, is surely enriching in shared feelings and experiences.

The challenge of affluence here, I think, is to individual values; only the individual can balance the material and the human aspects of his own existence.

In further explaining how we can best advance the human condition, I suggest that we need to keep a number of basic considerations immediately before us.

One is that population growth, unaccompanied by economic growth, results in a positive deterioration in the human condition.

Another is that people desire improved circumstances—and that these are desired especially by those millions around the world who have not yet participated in even those gains that relate directly to maintaining life and health.

Another is that regulation and restriction of growth do not automatically guarantee the preservation of scarce resources or an improved quality of life for people.

I am reminded here of these words by Valery Giscard d'Estaing, French prime minister, written when he was minister of Economics and Finance, in an article in *Preuves*:

> Should happiness lie in the possibility for the human mind to free itself from extreme material constraints and dedicate itself to an effort of culture and civilization, then I am convinced that the road we still have to cover in pursuit of economic growth is indeed one that takes us there, until we discover greatly expanded new horizons.[4]

Part III

—•*•—

ENERGY AND PROGRESS

CHAPTER 8

————•✳•————

Energy and the Petroleum Revolution

In 1959, on the occasion of the 100th anniversary of the founding of the American petroleum industry, I was privileged to participate in a symposium on "Energy and Man" sponsored by Columbia University. Among the other panel members who addressed the symposium was Allan Nevins, who discussed energy in the perspective of the history of western man. He expressed the significance of energy in these words:

> ... history is primarily the story of the increasing ability of man to reach and control energy. . . . Looking back on the centuries of muscle power and marveling at the pyramids, the walled palaces and cities, and the canals built by sheer animal energy, we easily ignore or forget the appalling limitations and hardships, the heartbreaking agonies, entailed by man's ignorance

93

of the stores of energy about him and of the means of utilizing them.[1]

The stark contrast between life in those early days of animal power and life in the latter half of the twentieth century testifies eloquently to the difference that energy development makes.

In the United States, for example, human labor today amounts to less than one percent of all the energy expended in our factories and other facilities for the production of goods and services. Machines fueled by petroleum, electricity generated from coal, and other forms of energy provide more than 99 percent of our power. Overall, Americans, who make up only 6 percent of the world's population, consume one-third of the world's annual output of fuel—about eight times as much per capita as the rest of the world.

This high rate of energy use is directly reflected in economic progress; for the people of the United States enjoy the highest average real income in the world. In fact, it is generally true that countries with the highest energy consumption have achieved the greatest economic advance. Underdeveloped countries which consume relatively small amounts of energy, such as India, Turkey and Brazil, also rank lowest in per capita income.

In the words of the Joint Economic Committee of the U.S. Congress, "energy is the ultimate raw material which permits the continued recycle of resources into most of man's requirements for food, clothing and shelter . . . the productivity of society is directly related to the per capita energy available."

Energy use in the United States has been rising steadily, with total consumption doubling between

1950 and 1970. Over a long period, however, industrial growth has been marked by technological developments which resulted in substantial gains in the efficiency of energy use. Outstanding examples of this were the development of the diesel engine, and the increasing efficiency of electric power generation. As a result, energy use has increased at a slower rate than real gross national product for most of this century.

However, in the latter half of the 1960s, energy consumption rose more rapidly than real gross national product, despite the broad economic shift away from manufacturing toward service industries that consume relatively less fuel. This reflected both an upsurge in consumption of energy for comfort and convenience, such as home air-conditioning, and an apparent decline in the efficiency of energy use. And it led to intensified demand pressures in the period of declining supply preceding the actual energy shortages of the early 1970s. Today, with prices up and conservation being emphasized, energy use is again rising more slowly than gross output.

The pattern of energy consumption in the United States has been marked by two major shifts in fuel sources. The first occurred in the latter half of the nineteenth century when coal replaced wood as the leading source of energy, rising from 9 percent of total national requirements in 1850 to 70 percent in 1900. Then, in the first half of the twentieth century, coal gave way to petroleum, with petroleum's contribution to total national energy needs rising from 9 percent in 1900 to 55 percent in 1950. Today petroleum—oil and natural gas—provides 77 percent of U.S. energy requirements, with the remainder supplied by coal, 18 percent; hydropower, 4 percent; and nuclear energy, approximately one percent.

Energy in America in the twentieth century is thus largely the story of petroleum and its development and widening use. For the first 70 years of the century, that story was one of plentiful supplies of fuel at relatively low costs. And the result was an economic growth thrust unprecedented in world history.

In the past several years, all of this has changed. A substantial gap has developed between domestic energy supply and demand, and America is experiencing for the first time ever in its peace-time history a scarcity of fuel. In the atmosphere of crisis that has developed with the realization of that shortage, the nation appears to be losing sight of the forces that provided its energy strength in the past. It is struggling to re-define its energy policies, and to get back on the road to an acceptable level of domestic self-sufficiency. In this situation, I think we have something to learn from the past achievements of the Americans who shaped the petroleum revolution.

That revolution is primarily a story of the wedding of American resourcefulness with the opportunities provided by a private enterprise system operating at full blast.

What that wedding achieved was far more than a simple proclamation that "we have found oil, it is cheap, have some."

Rather, under the thrust of competition, which was midwife at its birth, petroleum developed as an industry of great independence and vitality, as a restless innovator which continuously shook up the status quo. Its momentum started chain reactions extending into the technologies of other industries as well as directly into the everyday lives of everyday Americans. To say that the industry was bent on finding profitable markets for the rising tide of crude oil and natural gas, which it had learned to find and produce, is to say that it was bent upon turning its discoveries into products increasingly useful and appealing to people.

Its success is measured at least partially by the fact that Americans now depend upon petroleum for 77 percent of the energy they use. That number is a meaningful measure of petroleum's contribution to America's growth, but it is also grossly inexact. For one thing, it does not fully encompass the explosive effect on the economy of the mobility provided by the gasoline engine. Beyond that, where are the numbers that measure the significance of a carefully engineered lubrication system for high-speed machine tools powered by electricity generated by coal? Or the significance of the creation of whole new industries, some based upon raw materials from petroleum and others based on petroleum industry pressures for new and improved tools and materials? What I am suggesting is that petroleum is more than a source of energy and that the petroleum revolution sprang not just from the remarkable versatility of the hydrocarbon, but also from the dynamic nature of the industry itself.

The challenges posed by petroleum to man's resourcefulness were inherent in its physical location and nature.

The finding of a small oil sand by Colonel Drake in 1859 was the sheerest of accidents. The second man to drill found no oil; so it was early established that oil did not exist universally and that finding it was going to be the toughest prospecting job yet faced by man.

The early explorers relied on surface indications, hunch, the dowsing rod and even spiritualism. But that approach soon gave way to scientific method; and through a combination of the growing use of people trained in the earth sciences and the expenditure of many millions of dollars on research, petroleum exploration became a highly specialized science in its own right. Accordingly, scientific methods and instruments, ranging from geological analysis to the seismograph, are largely responsible for the more than 130 billion barrels of oil and vast supplies of gas so far located in the United States and sizable foreign reserves.

But there is still no technology that leads the explorer directly to petroleum. To find out for sure he must put his money on the line and drill. And when he does, he faces the fact that in high-risk exploratory drilling—in unproven territory—eight of nine U.S. wells are failures. Investing money in the face of those odds requires incentives, and wisely, the nation long provided incentives through the maintenance of a free market.

The need to perfect more precise methods of petroleum exploration remains a major industry challenge, one that Hollis M. Dole, formerly assistant secretary of the Department of the Interior, has referred to as "an urgent need to radically upgrade our techniques for finding the oil and gas which . . . awaits discovery here in the coterminous United States." And this is now a matter of intensive investigation.

Once oil was found, producing it presented new problems. Drake's well had to be pumped from the start. The first flowing wells came later and proved to be highly unpredictable. One produced 2,500 barrels daily for six months, and then went out like a light. Another was choked off by paraffin. In 1865, a nitroglycerine charge successfully boosted production in one well. But another operator who tried this wound up with a dry hole, while production in a competitor's neighboring well went up enormously. Such eccentricities provided an early introduction to some of the special perversities of nature. Obviously, there was much to learn about oil reservoirs, how to reach them, how to produce them and how to treat them to prolong their lives. A whole new specialization—petroleum engineering—grew up to concentrate on problems of this kind.

Through research, analysis and experimentation, although always dealing with unobservable phenomena as much as three or four miles underground, a vast body of knowledge has been developed. It is the foundation of present day oil and gas conservation laws, of techniques for assisted and secondary recovery and of unitized operation of oil fields in which all interests are pooled and entire reservoirs are produced on sound engineering principles as though under single ownership.

Improving oil recovery from producing reservoirs is one of the toughest challenges still facing the industry. It is estimated that over the entire time-span of U.S. petroleum operations, the recovery rate of discovered oil has averaged about 30 percent. Newer techniques have enabled the industry to push this figure far higher in individual cases, but the potential for further improvement is tremendous. Recovery is in part a function of cost, so the basic goal is to develop new methods that will enable a much larger proportion of oil in place to be recovered economically.

It was early established, too, that petroleum is migratory in nature. And this placed great competitive pressure on the oil man to produce, since if he failed to do so the oil or gas was likely to wind up in someone else's well. Once produced, it couldn't be piled up like wood or coal either, but had to be kept going. This pressure to keep oil moving is just as strong today as it was 100 years ago, and it makes ludicrous the charges that large volumes of oil have been held off the market to drive prices up.

Moving immense volumes of liquids and gases great distances posed additional problems for those Americans who pioneered petroleum development. They solved these by developing a specialized transportation system of their own, including the pipeline, tanker, tank car and tank truck. All of these not only contributed to broadening the availability of oil and reducing distribution costs, but also found application in other forms of enterprise—in moving coal slurry, molasses, chemicals and milk, for example.

Beyond the early distillation processes that were already known, petroleum refiners had their own challenges to meet. Lubrication became a science with the coming of petroleum. And with the aid of science, refiners began to design lubricants for an infinite variety of specialized applications. From here they went on to produce oils whose function was less to lubricate than to serve some other special purpose— for example, dielectric oils to insulate high-voltage transformers and processing oils which make rubber more workable and extend its supply by entering into and becoming an inseparable part of the rubber itself.

Another fundamental discovery came early in the second decade of this century. By 1915, gasoline demand exceeded that for kerosine. Even before that time, refiners bumped into the hard fact that nature had not put enough gasoline in crude oil to keep up with the soaring requirements of the automobile. In discovering how to break up oil fractions that were too heavy to burn in a gasoline engine, and thus increase gasoline yields, the way was found to effect a substantial increase in gasoline quality, too.

From this beginning the groundwork was laid for fuels for the high-compression engine, in itself a great contribution to economy in air and automotive transportation. The process which helped solve the immediate gasoline supply problem was thermal cracking patented in 1913. It was the first demonstration that the refiner could do more than separate his raw material; he could also transform it. The process was licensed for use by others at reasonable costs, setting a precedent highly significant in spreading advances in refining technology rapidly throughout the industry.

Oil refiners, spurred by the development of thermal cracking, launched research programs in earnest. More highly sophisticated processes for altering the characteristics of hydrocarbons followed thermal cracking. Notable among them were processes employing catalysts to promote and control reactions.

By World War II, the petroleum refiner had developed techniques capable of overcoming a dangerous under-supply of TNT, of creating a synthetic rubber industry almost overnight and of providing superior

101

aircraft performance for Allied forces through the production of prodigious quantities of aviation fuels of 100 octane quality and better.

Yet, as striking as these accomplishments were, it was in the postwar years that the amazing progress of petrochemistry became evident. Today the origin of some 3,000 organic chemicals can be traced back to crude oil and natural gas; and in some instances, the petroleum industry has become an important supplier of inorganic chemicals as well. Petrochemical manufacture is now a major industry, and the more than 600 petrochemical plants now operating in this country produce over half of the total volume of organic chemicals manufactured in the United States—using only 5 percent of domestic oil and gas production to accomplish this.

Petroleum refiners recognized over 50 years ago that their costs would go out of reach unless they operated large-capacity plants on a continuous flow basis and, in many respects, automatically. From that came the impetus for instrumentation theory; and for a dozen years beginning in the early 1920s, practically all industrial instruments, aside from instruments to measure and control electricity, flowed into the petroleum industry. The birth of the industrial instruments industry is more to be attributed to the petroleum refiner than to any other industrial group.

With the development of catalytic cracking in the 1930s, petroleum refiners needed instruments with built-in prescience—automatic controllers to handle programmed sequences of large numbers of interrelated changes. Thus they were in the forefront of automation, although they didn't know it for the word

102

had not yet been invented. The high degrees of automation being achieved in refining, as well as in production and pipeline operations, were simply matters
of taking steps which came naturally to attain the
results that had to be attained. The consequence of
this resourcefulness in penetrating the unknown was
low costs.

The operational innovations achieved by Americans
in shaping the petroleum industry were matched by
new forms of organization reflecting the special nature
of the business. Rather early a pattern of vertical integration emerged. This largely reflected the fact that
the unique, single-purpose facilities required for the
economical processing and handling of petroleum
involve substantial capital investment at levels of risk
which would be prohibitive in the absence of some
assurance of near-capacity rates of use. As demand
upon the industry grew, it became essential, if continuity of supply were to be maintained and economic
waste avoided, that the successive functions be integrated under a single corporate management or that
the result be sought through integration by contract.
As an economist might put it, there is great disutility
in a pipeline which has no source of supply or no
outlet.

Such organizational integration has often been
attacked as a nefarious scheme hatched for evil pur-
poses. It is demonstrable, however, that integration
first appeared not as a means of monopoly, but rather
as a weapon against monopoly. A refiner with assured
crude oil supplies and his own market outlets, for
example, was in a far better position to withstand the
onslaughts of a would-be monopolist than was the

refiner who was solely a refiner. An eminently desirable test of goodness or evil, in a society dedicated to the supremacy of the individual, is performance in the interest of the consuming public. Judged by that criterion, in terms of supply, price and user convenience, I think the record demonstrates that vertical integration scores high, indeed.

Among other things, integration facilitated the accumulation of capital resources committed to the great undertakings that have been necessary in seeking to maintain adequate supplies of petroleum. Even so, the largest of integrated companies have been too small to undertake alone the risks involved in many oil industry operations. Offshore leasing and drilling, deep exploratory tests of virgin territory such as Alaska's North Slope, construction of large-diameter long-distance pipelines, the development of oil abroad and, more recently, ventures into synthetic oil production are examples of what I am talking about.

As a consequence, many forms of risk-sharing have been developed and are common in the financial management of oil companies. These may range from a simple arrangement to pay a part of the cost of drilling a well—provided it proves to be a dry hole—to a full partnership in all costs and gains in exploring for oil in high-cost domestic or foreign areas or in synthetic fuel ventures.

Integration has also served consumers well on price. Gasoline is a fair test of performance here, since it has faced virtually no competition from alternative fuels. Through the year 1972—prior to the severe shortages that boosted prices sharply in 1973 and 1974—gasoline prices had traditionally lagged behind those of consumer items generally. Too far behind, in fact, since federal control of oil and natural gas prices held those prices at levels below those required for adequate profitability.

As a result, gasoline was selling at retail in 1972 for 24½ cents per gallon excluding direct taxes, a full penny a gallon below the average price back in 1920. Moreover, the quality of the 1972 gasoline on an octane basis was at least 50 percent better.

Since 1972, prices have increased sharply due to continuing inflation and to rising imported oil prices dictated by foreign governments.

Basic to all that I have said here about the petroleum revolution is the thesis, first, that petroleum presented great challenges in science, technology, organization and finance. Secondly, these challenges were accepted because the incentive and freedom to do so existed. Thirdly, the resourcefulness with which the challenges were met had a multiplying effect in contributing to the well-being of mankind. And, finally, the performance of the petroleum industry is a testament to the efficiency of a system of maximum individual liberty and minimum governmental license in promoting economic progress.

Unfortunately, in some key respects this is the world that was. Back in 1959, when the petroleum industry was marking its 100th birthday, there were already indications that the climate was changing. And I remember concluding my address at the Columbia symposium in that year with these words:

> . . . there are aspects of the future which are clouded by the penetration of non-economic forces into the functioning of an industry which

has always performed best in an atmosphere of economic freedom. The course of the second 100 years of the petroleum revolution depends, I believe, upon the extent to which the atmosphere of economic freedom is preserved in America.[2]

In the 15 years since then, freedom and incentive have been eroded. As a result, the United States now finds itself for the first time in history facing real, turn-down-the-thermostat, line-up-for-gasoline energy shortages—shortages that it must learn to live with for a considerable period into a future that will be marked by heavy dependency on foreign oil.

CHAPTER 9

———— ✳ ————

The Anatomy of a Crisis

AMERICANS are likely to long remember 1973 as the start of a new energy era in the United States. For 1973 was the year in which an emerging recognition of energy scarcity was suddenly transformed into the conscious reality of energy shortage. With startling swiftness, the outbreak of war in the Middle East, the cutback in oil production there and the embargoing of shipments to this country dramatized, as nothing earlier had, the changed energy situation of the United States.

In brief, the nation had come up short on domestic energy and was now perilously dependent on imported fuel that could—and would—be denied to it by foreign governments.

The basic problem that came into focus then was not the loss of Middle East oil—although that itself was troublesome—but the widening gap between domestic energy supply and domestic energy demand. This problem had been building for many years from decisions made and actions taken much earlier. But it burst upon the American consciousness with explosive impact in 1973.

The root of the problem was that we had given top priority to too many objectives. We wanted energy to be plentiful and we wanted it to be cheap. We wanted it to be secure—there when we needed it. We wanted it to be clean, to be pumped from the ground, processed into products and used by the public without affecting the environment. We wanted new investment to expand energy supply and we wanted more taxes from the energy suppliers.

There were other things we didn't want: No drilling or offshore terminals, or refineries or nuclear power plants, in our neighborhoods, for example.

These "wants" and "don't wants" collided in the decade of the 1960s and a crack opened in the armor of our self-reliance in energy supply. I recall warning of the trouble ahead in a speech I delivered in 1967, following the crisis in world oil supply that grew out of fighting in the Middle East that year. On that occasion, the Suez Canal was blocked by sunken ships. Middle East pipelines were blown up and the world was suddenly short almost 10 million barrels of oil per day. In an unrelated coincidence, civil war broke out in Nigeria and blockage of its oil ports cut off another half million barrels of daily oil supply.

In four months of 1967—June through September —the United States shipped nearly 24 million barrels of crude oil to other Free World nations and overcame a deficiency of 27 million barrels in its own Middle East imports. At the same time, American oil companies achieved dramatic increases in production in Iran, Venezuela and other non-Arab countries of the Free World to rescue Europe and Japan from critical situations.

This massive disruption was scarcely noticed in the United States. But it was clear to me, and to many other American oil men, that another emergency of that character would find us extremely vulnerable. So in my 1967 speech I called attention to the declining discovery rate of new oil and gas reserves in the United States and the reasons for it:

> On the one hand, rising costs. On the other, the depressing effect of natural gas controls on fuel oil and crude oil prices and the overhanging threat of government retaliation if gasoline prices are raised. . . .
>
> As a consequence of insufficient incentive, domestic production adequate to meet consumption requirements in the years ahead is unlikely. Unless there is a change in the economic climate in which our industry operates, and soon, we face the stark fact that the last crisis we met with distinction was the last crisis we will be *capable* of meeting with distinction.[1]

The following year, the United States passed the point of being physically able to meet its oil needs. And by 1973 the gap between domestic oil production and consumption had widened to more than 6 million barrels—252 million gallons—of oil daily, and was still growing.

That gap was compounded by a number of developments critical to U.S. petroleum supply—by reduced incentives for searching out new supplies of oil and gas; by growing government regulation that impinged increasingly on profitability; by rising taxes; by a crunch in the supply of capital for energy development; and by steadily rising demand for energy by Americans and the American economy.

If it were possible to select a precise time at which the forces which produced America's energy crisis were set in motion, that time would be June 7, 1954. On that date the United States Supreme Court, in the landmark Phillips Petroleum decision, ruled that producers of natural gas sold in interstate commerce were subject to the provisions of the Natural Gas Act of 1938. That Act was designed to regulate interstate gas pipeline companies as public utilities and, by its own language, exempted gas producers from such regulation.

The court's rationale for declaring otherwise was a need for "protection of consumers against exploitation by natural gas companies." Thus, by court decision, rather than legislation, all natural gas going into interstate commerce was subjected to price and other controls at the wellhead.

The decision was widely hailed as a victory for consumers. But there were dissenters, including petroleum industry officials, who saw it as a hollow victory, indeed, and who warned that the nation was courting serious difficulties in future energy supply. That view proved to be precisely correct, for the court's 1954 decision marked a turning point in the U.S. petroleum energy supply situation. What happened after 1954 stands in stark contrast to the achievements of the previous 10 years—and the half century before that.

A period of dynamic expansion followed the ending of World War II, with production of crude oil and natural gas liquids rising from 5 million barrels daily in 1946 to 7.6 million barrels daily in 1955. This level of output exceeded by some 2 million barrels daily the industry's own estimate of what it had earlier thought possible. And, over the same period, the industry generated an unused production capacity of 1.8 million barrels daily—a surplus of more than 20 percent above actual production volumes.

This expansion clearly stemmed from rising crude oil prices, which more than doubled during the two years after they were freed from wartime controls, rising from $1.22 to $2.60 per barrel. In effect, a doubling of price resulted in almost doubling supply.

Following the imposition of natural gas prices controls in 1954, the petroleum situation changed drastically. Regulation of gas prices impacted on oil prices, too, since oil and gas frequently compete in the same markets. This pressure, coupled with federal surveillance of oil prices under the mandatory import control program, led to predictable results.

The real price of domestic crude oil (expressed in constant 1973 dollars) declined from $4.77 per barrel in 1954 to $3.89 per barrel in 1973. And the composite price of both crude oil and natural gas at the wellhead declined from $3.19 per barrel to $2.26 per barrel over the same period.

The impact on supply of this declining price trend was not long in coming. Caught between controlled prices and steadily rising costs, and fully aware of the long-shot odds in wildcat drilling, petroleum companies were forced to become increasingly selective in exploratory ventures.

Exploratory drilling fell from a high of more than 16,000 wells in 1956 to a low of 6,922 wells in 1971. Proved reserves of both oil and natural gas in the "lower 48" states peaked in 1967, and have declined each year since then. Measured against production, available oil reserves dropped from a 14-year supply in 1954 to an 8-year supply in 1973, and gas reserves fell from a 22-year to an 10-year supply.

Further, the reserve-producing capacity of some 2 million barrels daily built up earlier in the postwar period had largely disappeared by 1972.

As demand continued to rise in the face of lagging production and reserves, the United States turned increasingly to what was then lower-cost foreign oil. When natural gas price control was imposed in 1954, this country depended upon foreign sources for 13 percent of its oil needs. By 1968, when the United States was no longer physically able to meet its domestic oil requirements from domestic production, this figure had climbed to 21 percent. And in 1973, prior to the embargo, foreign oil was meeting approximately 36 percent of United States petroleum requirements.

At the heart of this deterioration in domestic energy development was a severe erosion of petroleum industry profitability. This was particularly severe in the five-year period from 1968 through 1972. Over that period, petroleum earnings as a percentage of stockholders' equity declined each year, falling to a 10-year low of 10.8 percent in 1972.

112

The fact that all manufacturing companies averaged a return of 12.1 percent in that same year attests to the depressed level of petroleum profits. Further, according to a First National City Bank of New York survey, the petroleum industry trailed 26 other manufacturing industries in profitability. Among those earning higher rates of return were the automobile, chemical, drug, printing and publishing, tobacco and appliance industries. And none of these, to my knowledge, faces risks even approaching those faced by petroleum companies in searching for new supplies of oil and natural gas. For example, over the past 15 years, only one in each 51 exploratory wells drilled in the United States found enough oil or gas to be commercially successful.

At the same time that depressed prices were taking a heavy toll in profitability, pressures were building for tax changes that would further slash earnings. These culminated in the Tax Reform Act of 1969 which boosted petroleum taxes by some $500 million each year. Since these dollars would pay for drilling some 5,000 average exploratory wells annually, the impact on the petroleum search was severe.

As the domestic petroleum supply situation steadily worsened, U.S. demand for oil and gas steadily grew.

In broad perspective, this reflected a growing population, a rising level of affluence and, reflecting that affluence, increasing convenience and recreational uses of energy. Gasoline demand rose at a particularly fast rate, as new car sales continued at a brisk pace and as buyers increasingly sought power options that eat up more fuel. Ninety percent of all cars produced in the early 1970s had automatic transmissions, for example, and close to 70 percent had air conditioning.

In the absence of any other consideration, this burgeoning demand was exerting heavy pressures on petroleum supply. But there were other considerations; and when new requirements were imposed on an already shaky energy balance, the supply situation rapidly became critical.

The new pressures on petroleum supply emerging during the 1960s stemmed primarily from America's growing concern for the environment. The nation's efforts to clean up pollution where it already existed, and to prevent new environmental damage in the future, significantly boosted energy consumption while at the same time restricting the development of new supplies.

On the demand side, an extraordinary acceleration in petroleum use resulted from efforts to comply with new air quality standards legislated by government, with auto emission controls exacting a heavy penalty in gasoline mileage.

The effort to comply with air quality standards also sharply boosted demand for distillate fuel oil. To meet sulfur emission restrictions, utilities began to substitute oil for coal and to mix low-sulfur distillate with high-sulfur residual oils. Overall, the use of distillates for the generation of electricity doubled from 1971 to 1972. Consumption of low-sulfur residual oil climbed substantially, too.

On the other side of the equation, concern for the environment created this paradox: While the U.S. was struggling to make ends meet on fuels, the largest oil field ever discovered in the Western Hemisphere lay untapped. This is the Prudhoe Bay Field on Alaska's North Slope, discovered in 1968 and estimated to contain some 10 billion barrels of oil and 26 trillion cubic feet of natural gas. Delays in developing the field stemmed from fears that building a trans-Alaska pipeline would lead to grave environmental damage.

Congressional action in 1973 cleared the way for construction of the line. But the oil that was earlier expected to get to market in 1972 will not be available until late 1977 at the earliest. And the impact of that kind of uncertainty on supply planning is obvious. The delay had a significant side effect, too, in discouraging further exploration for new discoveries on the Slope.

Large oil deposits in the Santa Barbara Channel off California also await development. A moratorium on drilling was imposed there because of feared environmental damage, even though scientific studies have shown no evidence of permanent harm from a 1969 oil spill in the Channel. Environmental challenges have also slowed development of petroleum resources elsewhere on the outer continental shelf, potentially the best hope for major U.S. discoveries.

Concern for the environment has also been a factor in lagging U.S. refining capacity. Basically, the impact of depressed product prices in limiting profitability made refining expansion a singularly unattractive proposition during the latter half of the 1960s and early 1970s. But beyond this, a high level of uncertainty about the future availability of crude oil discouraged new construction, as did rising environmental opposition to the siting of refineries in coastal and other areas. The National Petroleum Refiners Association has identified 20 empty refinery sites where land was acquired and refinery construction permits were sought in vain. By the close of 1973, the nation's total refining capacity was trailing actual oil consumption by more than 3 million barrels daily. And in 1974, large volumes of projected new capacity were being cancelled due primarily to allocation regulations and price controls.

Two other developments adding to oil requirements are the continuing shortage of natural gas and the lag in bringing nuclear power facilities on stream. So severe was the gas shortage after 20 years of federal regulation that interstate pipeline companies were forced to curtail deliveries by 1,250 billion cubic feet over the 12-month period ending in March, 1974.

The nuclear power expectations of the 1960s simply failed to materialize. In 1968, for example, the Department of the Interior projected an anticipated capacity of 57,000 megawatts of electricity to be generated from nuclear reactors by 1973, based on plants in operation or planned. But in 1973 less than one-third of the estimated capacity was in operation. And nuclear power was providing less than one percent of U.S. energy requirements.

All of this culminated in the energy shortages that hit the United States full-force in 1973. During that year, natural gas was denied to those seeking new service in many parts of the country, shortages of heating oil developed and gasoline supplies were tight. The embargoing of Middle East oil late in the year, coming atop the already tight-as-a-drum energy balance, threatened the nation with damaging shortages and led to the adoption of comprehensive fuel conservation measures and a system of oil allocation.

By early 1974, the full impact of the embargo was being felt in the United States and oil supplies were running about 13 percent below pre-embargo estin.ates of demand. The combination of conservation measures and unusually warm weather enabled the nation to get through the heating season without serious damage, but gasoline shortages were severe in some sections of the country. Lifting of the embargo in March then eased the immediate supply problem. But the outlook for continuing restrictions on production by the Arab nations and the size of the domestic energy gap made it clear that American consumers were facing energy scarcity for years into the future.

It was also clear in 1973 that Americans were going to have to pay more for their energy supplies. Rising costs were pushing domestic oil prices to higher levels, and ever higher prices were being dictated by foreign governments for oil shipped into this country. U.S. crude was selling at an average price of $6.50 per barrel in early 1974, while Persian Gulf postings exceeded $11 per barrel and spot market prices were still higher. The rolling in of higher costs for imported oil with rising domestic costs pushed U.S. product prices to new high levels. Gasoline, for example, was selling as high as 60 cents per gallon in the early months of 1974.

Rising prices improved profitability, which was precisely what was needed to stimulate the development of new U.S. supplies. Nonetheless, the improved profits were sharply attacked by critics who pictured the industry as profiteering from the energy shortage.

The fact is, however, that petroleum industry profits for 1973 averaged just a 15.6 percent return on stockholders' equity. This was only modestly above the 14.8 percent return earned by manufacturing companies generally and *trailed* the returns for nine other industries.

In the face of the factual record of growing energy scarcity and the reasons for it, the myth lives on that the crisis in energy was contrived by the petroleum industry. While the industry could be faulted for its earlier failure to recognize how quickly a critical shortage would develop, it cannot be faulted for the quality of its response in seeking to meet America's energy needs with a minimum of supply disruptions. And it surely did not contrive the price controls, the environmental regulations and the restrictions on off-shore petroleum development that resulted in energy shortages.

Still, in 1974, many Americans harbored considerable doubt and suspicion about energy problems. According to opinion survey results, 62 percent of the public believed that oil companies were holding back on supply. And 68 percent said they were not satisfied with industry efforts to relieve the shortages. And 55 percent—more than half of all Americans—expressed doubt that the energy supply problem is a long-term problem.

This is a clear warning, in my opinion, that sensationalism and looseness in dealing with the facts is a divisive influence on Americans. It is particularly harmful at a time when, in their own interests, they need to be pulling together. And it is also a virtual guarantee of delay and error in dealing with the problems of energy.

Delay and error we can ill afford for our problems are real and immediate. And we must face up now to hard decisions on policies for the future that are essential to the accelerated development of domestic energy resources.

CHAPTER 10

———◆◆———

Energy for the Future

In the atmosphere of crisis and recrimination that has marked the dawning of a new energy era in the United States, the process of shaping new national fuels policies has been slow and painful. We have been unable to agree on goals. We have had difficulty in distinguishing clearly between areas for public action and those for private action. And we have failed to realize that we are dealing not just with one energy problem but with a series of separate but closely interrelated problems that reach far beyond fuel supplies.

There are, for example, basic problems of energy development. But there are also interwoven environmental problems. Foreign policy problems. Technological problems. Financial problems. Conservation problems. And very real problems relating to public knowledge and understanding.

120

Attempting to deal with these on an individual basis, in the absence of clearly defined goals and priorities, has crippled the national response to the energy challenge. We have bogged down in a swamp of crisis, confrontation and conflicting political moves.

Our failure to resolve the issues entails a high degree of risk to the economic and military security of the United States. And it is vital that we reappraise our energy situation now to identify the actions that must be taken to assure essential fuel supplies for the future.

A starting point in this reappraisal is a recognition of the fact that there is no shortage of basic energy resources to be developed in the United States. The Department of the Interior has made this point very clearly in these words:

> Our Nation has been bountifully endowed with a large resource base of fuel minerals, which includes petroleum, natural gas, coal, oil shale, uranium and thorium. The energy content of known resources of these fuel minerals amounts to 13,100 quadrillion Btu's, enough to last 190 years at the rate of consumption in 1970.
>
> The potential resources of fuel minerals that are on the verge of use but await technologic advance will last 16,500 years at the rate of energy use in 1970. A major national objective, then, is to identify and delineate these resources and to develop the technology for utilizing them as they are needed.[1]

Of key importance to the immediate outlook is the fact that most of our petroleum reserves are yet to be found. The National Petroleum Council has estimated that 55 percent of the discoverable oil and 66 percent of the discoverable natural gas in this country are still in the ground. This potential for new discoveries is encouraging, since we will be heavily dependent upon oil and natural gas in the years immediately ahead.

Our problem then is not a lack of energy resources, but a need to develop the resources we have. And this leads directly to consideration of our national energy goals.

There is a considerable range of opinion about what we should strive for in domestic resource development. At one extreme, some urge that in the interests of resource conservation and minimum environmental disruption, domestic energy resources should be developed and used as sparingly as possible. This would be made possible by a combination of heavy U.S. reliance on imported fuels and severe restraints on fuel consumption.

Serious questions arise in considering this position. These include the resulting vulnerability of the U.S. economy to foreign supply interruptions, the fairness of "exporting" environmental disruptions to other countries and the impact of proposed energy use restrictions on the quality of life in America.

At the other extreme is the position taken by the U.S. government in first preparing Project Independence. The goal of this project, in brief, was complete energy independence for the United States by 1980, with this country becoming a net exporter of energy in subsequent years. The route to obtaining such independence would be all-out development of conventional and synthetic fuel resources here at home.

While this position is understandable in terms of recent energy supply difficulties, I suggest that it is neither capable of achievement in terms of acceptable

122

costs nor a desirable objective in terms of the long-run interests of the people of the United States and the world.

From a practical standpoint, there is simply not enough time between now and 1980 to find and develop the petroleum, build the nuclear power capacity and bring into commercial production the synthetic fuels that would be required to give the United States energy independence.

Even if this were possible, it would be undesirable. For the concept of "going it alone" is directly contrary to the philosophy of mutually benefitting trade among the nations of the world. And to the extent that it would be viewed by others as the embracing of a kind of economic fortress America, it would represent a retrogression in our international relationships.

It is quite possible, also, that seeking the goal of complete energy independence could lock Americans and the American economy into an unnecessarily high-cost energy supply situation. Or, alternatively, it could leave a developing U.S. synthetic fuels industry high and dry as a result of the unrestrained competition of lower-cost foreign fuels.

In my view, the energy goals of the United States should be shaped on the basis of the following considerations.

One, we should accelerate the development of our domestic resources both to meet our own requirements and to contribute to world energy needs in a period of tightening supply.

Two, in doing so we should work toward building a domestic energy production capability that, in combination with fuels imported from nearby and reliable sources, would permit us to meet our essential energy needs in time of emergency.

Three, at the same time, we should continue to fulfill our energy requirements as economically as possible from both domestic and foreign sources within the normal patterns of world trade.

The large-scale development of domestic resources that will be required is an achievable goal, but not an easily achievable one. It will require the willingness to assume risks, vast amounts of capital and major technological advance. It will also require a judicious blend of private and public action, and the discipline that restricts each to its proper area of activity. Here there is grave concern for the future. For in the environment of 1974, it is not unimaginable that we will lose sight of what has been accomplished by the private sector in the past and turn to government for solutions that government cannot provide.

Despite the unmistakable warnings of deterioration in our domestic energy supply situation under the onus of federal regulation, strong forces both inside government and without are today seeking further and punitive restrictions on private energy development.

Legislation before the 93rd Congress called for such actions as breaking up integrated petroleum companies, requiring federal chartering of oil companies, empowering the Federal Power Commission to control oil prices, regulating the petroleum industry as a public utility and establishing a federal oil and gas corporation to search for and develop new oil and gas reserves.

What these proposals really represent are the initial steps in the nationalization of the petroleum industry, and they should be appraised precisely on that basis. For they promise nothing in the way of a strengthened energy position for the United States.

To achieve our longer-term goal of energy security as economically as possible, past experience suggests that we free our private enterprise economy to function. This will require that we take specific action in relation to both short-term and long-term considerations.

Looking at the short-term first, the top priority is termination of petroleum price controls. The fact that controls discourage the development of new petroleum reserves has been documented. Data published in 1974 show that the decline in reserves is continuing, with crude oil reserves dropping by one billion barrels in 1973 and gas reserves falling by 16 trillion cubic feet.

Decontrol of prices is widely supported by economists, including many who have no association with the petroleum industry. M. A. Adelman, professor of economics at MIT and frequently a severe critic of the industry, has commented as follows on the reasons for natural gas supply shortages:

> The mistake was in not letting the market for natural gas adjust to changes, which is the chief social purpose of setting up a market system in the first place. . . . For years some tried to persuade themselves and the rest of us that natural gas production was really not a competitive market, but fortunately that argument has been so discredited as no longer to need discussion.[2]

It is significant that even the easing of controls on prices in 1973 quickly resulted in an upswing in petroleum exploration.

Second, our nation must maintain an economic climate that will enable the energy industries to generate and attract the vast sums of capital they will require. This means, most importantly, that the increased profits essential to energy development not be siphoned off in taxes, as in the proposed repeal of percentage depletion and "excess" profits levy that would boost oil taxes by some $3 billion in 1975.

Future energy development now shapes up as one of the greatest investment challenges in history.

In the comprehensive study completed in 1972, the National Petroleum Council suggested that the total capital requirements of the domestic energy industries would amount to more than $500 billion over the 1971 to 1985 period (in 1970 dollars). This is equivalent to some $34 billion annually—substantially more if inflation is taken into account. Helping to put this figure into perspective is the fact that the entire Apollo space program cost in the range of $25 billion. So the domestic energy industries must invest funds equivalent to one and one-half Apollo programs for each year of the 15-year period.

Within this total picture, the Council further suggested that the petroleum industry alone would require more than $250 billion over the period for investment in conventional and synthetic fuels development. This works out to an average annual investment of some $17 billion, without allowing for inflation, which is more than double the average for the previous decade.

On a broader basis, the Chase Manhattan Bank has estimated that worldwide petroleum industry financial requirements will amount to a staggering $1,350 billion over the period 1970 to 1985. Some $450 billion of this represents capital required for exploration and development of conventional oil and gas supplies.

Since more than half of these capital needs must be generated in profits, it is essential that the 1973 and 1974 improvement in profitability be maintained.

A third required action is the striking of a new and more realistic balance between environmental and energy objectives. Environmental concerns have impacted seriously on energy supply through blocking the Alaska pipeline, restricting offshore development and impeding the siting of refineries and nuclear power plants. They are also blocking the broader utilization of our vast coal reserves, which are the key to immediate large-scale expansion of domestic fuel supply. An immediate need is the temporary modification of regulations where necessary to permit the full utilization of all available fuel resources. And then we must work toward a balance that weighs costs as well as benefits in arriving at policies that will permit sound progress toward both environmental and energy goals.

Fourth, we must look also at the demand side of the domestic energy equation in a searching reappraisal of our approach to energy use.

There is no question but that we have used energy wastefully in the past and that we must discipline ourselves to more sparing use in the future. Having to pay prices that more nearly reflect today's energy development costs will help us to save fuel in such day-to-day uses as personal transportation, heating and air conditioning. But beyond that we will be required to face up to some major technical challenges, such as learning to generate electricity more efficiently, and to some significant changes in life-styles, such as widespread use of mass-transit facilities, smaller and less powerful automobiles and comprehensive recycling programs for materials that require heavy energy consumption in initial production.

While we work to improve our domestic energy balance by expanding supply and restraining the growth in consumption, we need to keep an overriding reality in mind: The degree of energy self-sufficiency and security we seek is not immediately available.

We are playing catch-up ball, and energy development takes time. So, we must continue to rely heavily on imported oil, and we must continue to have access to foreign supplies. Further, we need to diversify our foreign sources as rising world demand intensifies pressures on available supply and as large foreign producers talk increasingly of production restrictions.

This requires that U.S. energy policy recognize the need for continuing participation of American companies in foreign petroleum development and for the investment of large amounts of capital abroad. Particularly, it requires that U.S. tax treatment of foreign income continue to be geared to permitting U.S. companies to compete on an equal basis with foreign competitors.

My own company's experience demonstrates the growing short-term importance of foreign oil in the U.S. supply picture. Sun is primarily a domestic company, with its investment base largely concentrated in North America. Even so, it has been necessary for us in the past decade to move increasingly into foreign petroleum exploration. We have been forced to do

128

this in an effort to acquire additional crude oil supplies for our refineries, since domestic petroleum exploration opportunities were limited. If U.S. policy changed to make it uneconomic for us to continue our foreign exploration efforts, or to make it impossible to compete with foreign companies, the result would be less-secure crude for our refineries and less product for our U.S. customers.

Domestic petroleum needs are not the sole reason for U.S. participation in foreign petroleum development, however. U.S. companies also play a major role in helping to make petroleum fuels available to the developing nations whose economic progress depends heavily on rising energy use. And the combination of accelerated development of our own resources, which will ease the pressure on oil supplies outside the United States, and our continuing participation in foreign energy development should demonstrate our commitment to a mutually beneficial approach to world energy matters.

Shifting to the longer-term outlook, the commercial production of synthetic fuels from our vast domestic resources is our primary task.

When we talk high-volume synthetic fuel operations, we are talking essentially about production of gas from coal and liquid fuels from coal and oil shale deposits. Time, money and technology are the keys to unlocking these energy storehouses. Costly research and heavy capital investments will be required for new processes, equipment technology, pilot operations and, ultimately, commercial-scale facilities. And still we are unlikely to see significant results in terms of new energy supply until the decade of the 1980s.

Coal is our most abundant fossil fuel, with total resources estimated at 3.2 trillion tons. Converting some of this into gas is the most promising prospect for substantial additions to our fuel supplies in the next 10 years. Pilot plants are now in operation, and two commercial-scale plants using proven technology have been announced and could be in production by the latter years of this decade. This will be a high-Btu product that can be moved through pipelines to supplement natural gas.

Also under study in coal technology are production of a low-Btu gas that could be burned at the conversion site to produce low-cost electricity and the extraction from coal of synthetic oil that could be refined into a range of products.

One of America's largest energy resources is the Green River oil shale formation spreading across Colorado, Utah and Wyoming. The shale yields kerogen, which can be refined into gasoline and other products. Total reserves are estimated at 1.8 trillion barrels, and the National Petroleum Council estimates that 129 billion barrels are minable with present technology.

Construction engineering is under way on a 46,000 barrels daily plant, with operations scheduled to begin in 1976-77, and research on retorting technology is being carried forward.

Major new impetus for the shale oil development effort was provided by the initiation of a federal prototype leasing program in January 1974. The government, which owns some 80 percent of oil shale lands, established the program to encourage development

activity and to obtain data on economic and environmental costs.

Tar sands—sand impregnated with heavy oil—occur
in 14 of the United States. Although they are generally of poor quality, in total they represent a sizable
energy resource. However, the bulk of potential tar
sands oil is contained in the rich Athabasca and other
sands to the north in Alberta Province, Canada. Total
reserves there are estimated at 330 billion barrels of
bitumen, which could yield a synthetic crude oil output of 250 billion barrels.

Sun Oil Company has been operating in Alberta
since the late 1960s the world's first—and so far, only
—commercial plant for the production of synthetic
crude oil from tar sands. And our experience there is
indicative, I think, of the challenges that will be faced
in bringing synthetic fuels from other sources into
commercial production.

The facilities were completed in 1967, and initial
operations commenced in the fall of that year. We ran
into trouble immediately, with an almost complete
failure of our boiler and power generation system and
with serious difficulties in winter mining of the sands.
It was not until 1969 that we completed a full year of
commercial production.

These early operating problems, combined with the
low price of crude oil, led to heavy losses in the early
years of operation. As a result, the present financial picture is that we have invested over $300 million in the
project and have lost an additional $70 million to date.
Or to put it another way, adding 45,000 barrels daily
of high-quality synthetic crude oil production to North
America's energy supply required a massive investment

of funds on which no profit had been earned through 1973. And close to 10 years was required from the initial planning to commercial operation.

The extent to which future oil production from the Athabasca sands will help to meet U.S. needs will be determined, of course, by Canadian government policies. It is likely, however, that the export market will be an important consideration in development of the tar sands.

Beyond synthetic fuels, there is a tremendous potential for developing new supplies of energy from other sources.

Geothermal energy—"earth heat" in the form of steam and hot water—is already being used to produce low-cost electricity in northern California. And exploration programs for new sources are being carried out in a number of western states.

Nuclear power offers the prospect of the breeder reactor, which produces its own fuel supplies at the same time that it gives off heat to produce electricity, and a potential energy utopia based upon nuclear fusion. Fusion would use abundantly available fuels in a process free of radioactive waste to produce virtually limitless supplies of energy.

The ultimate in energy resources, of course, is the sun, and the long-range promise is conversion of solar energy into electricity. There are a variety of other potential energy sources, too, ranging from the burning of trash in power plants to windmills on open water. All could contribute to meeting future fuel needs.

In brief, America's long-term power prospects are bright, indeed, despite present problems. The nation has vast resources of energy. And it has in abundance the human resourcefulness, the capital and the technological capacity that are required to develop and to harness that energy to man's needs. What is needed is the political-economic climate that will encourage the commitment of human and capital resources to fuels development and the freedom that will permit those resources to be used innovatively and effectively in the service of society.

Part IV

—•—

PERSPECTIVES:
BUSINESS TOMORROW

IT is paradoxical today that at the high point of its contributions to American society, U.S. business is being written off by some as a declining force that will be subordinate in the future to government and other institutions.

While the business community may protest that this report of its demise is greatly exaggerated, the fact remains that very serious questions have arisen about the nature and role of business in the future. And it is essential that those questions be closely examined today, as a prerequisite to helping to define a coming role that will continue the responsiveness of business to the needs of society as business newly perceives them.

In assessing the present situation, this fact stands out in bold relief:

Business has failed to gain public understanding of the nature of the vast change it has undergone in

137

recent decades in relation to organization, management, human relationships and sensitivity to society's needs. As a result, people tend to continue to see business in the stereotypes of 50 years ago—as a rigid, authoritarian institution with a single orientation: dollar profits. The result is a low level of public support for business and a tendency to view the private enterprise system as one incapable of functioning effectively in the complex environment of today.

Reflecting this, views of the future range all the way from nationalization of a number of basic industries (legislation calling for precisely this for the petroleum industry is now before Congress) to the expectation that major economic decision-making will gradually pass from the corporation to government with business performing primarily in a technician role.

There are both short-term and long-term considerations for business in assessing its present situation and future role relative to these expectations.

Looking at the short-term first, there is considerable ambivalence today in public attitudes toward business. On the one hand, most Americans seem to realize that business is good at solving problems and getting things done. And this is reflected in the fact that many want business to move beyond its traditional sphere of operations and take a hand in solving the nation's pressing social problems.

On the other hand, the public has in recent years become increasingly critical of the *motives* of American business. This is particularly significant in that it represents a reversal of the trend prevalent during the past two decades.

Back in the 1930s, there was considerable disenchantment with the business system during the years of depression and slow and uneven economic recovery. In the expansion following World War II, these basic attitudes changed substantially, with the performance of business earning a high degree of public support. But that support is now eroding, according to public opinion surveys.

The Yankelovich research organization reports, for example, that only one American in three agrees that business tries to strike a fair balance between profits and the public interest. And two Americans in three say business is overly concerned with profit at the expense of the public interest, that business has "too much" power and that it should be controlled and regulated more to prevent its taking advantage of consumers and from exerting too much influence on our government's foreign and domestic policies.

Such public attitudes toward private companies are contributing, in my opinion, to some of the very serious problems that business faces today. An outstanding example of this is the plight of Consolidated Edison, which is experiencing a financial crisis due to a lack of public and governmental support in its efforts to deal with New York City's power problems. Environmentalist opposition to building new generating capacity in and around New York City, high taxes on service and strong consumer resistance to needed rate increases—extending even to refusal to pay current bills for service—has placed the giant utility in an untenable position.

The lack of public support for business reflects in part, I think, a lack of knowledge of basic economics and how our business system works. But it reflects something more, too. And that is the failure of business to communicate in a meaningful way to the public, with the result that its credibility has now reached a disastrously low level.

A part of the credibility problem lies in the difficulties experienced by the press and broadcast media in reporting and interpreting increasingly complex economic and operational developments and issues. Creed Black, editor of the Philadelphia Inquirer, has commented to me on the extreme complexity of the energy issue, adding that "I don't think I've ever found a story harder to get a handle on." But business must bear a substantial share of the blame, too, and dealing with the problem is going to require some very specific actions by U.S. businessmen.

One is that we are going to have to be more open and candid in releasing information about our operations.

Another is that we must demonstrate a greater sense of personal accountability for the actions of our organizations.

Another is that we must more fully consider the long-range social and economic implications of our actions. In the petroleum industry, for example, resource conservation and the most efficient possible utilization of scarce capital in the development of new supplies of energy are of paramount importance. And the future business strategies and operations of the petroleum industry must accord with these overriding considerations.

In the longer-range perspective, the continued existence of private enterprise in its present form is being questioned by academic-intellectual observers. Basically, they suggest that business generally and the corporation specifically are heading into a period of declining importance in American society. Some argue that the increasing complexity of society's problems requires that government rather than the market wield decision-making power; others say that the corporation has been tried and found wanting in the area of generating social progress; and others argue that the concentration of corporate interest on creating "frivolous desires" unrelated to real human satisfactions is unacceptable for the future.

Perhaps the most comprehensive picture of an anticipated future emerges from Daniel Bell's description of the "post-industrial society." Mr. Bell, a Harvard sociologist, argues that continuing rapid change will be reflected in the decline of the corporation as a "central force" in American life.

The U.S. economy will become largely a service as opposed to a manufacturing economy, as a smaller and smaller proportion of the labor force is required to produce the physical goods we need. We will become a knowledge society, with a new class of highly skilled professionals and technicians. Knowledge will become the source of growth and change, and the "knowledge institute"—university or other research-based organization—will supplant the corporation as the dominant organization of the next 100 years. Scientists, engineers and economists will constitute an intellectual technology in the post-industrial society; and major economic decisions will be made through government rather than left to the market. Private companies will execute the plans and decisions that are made, but they will lose much of the freedom they now enjoy to choose how they grow.

The implications of this kind of society are summed up by Bell in these words:

> To say that the major institutions of the new society will be intellectual is to say that production and business decisions will be subordinated to, or will derive from, other forces in society; that the crucial decisions regarding the growth of the economy and its balance will come from government, but they will be based on the government's sponsorship of research and development, of cost effectiveness and cost-benefit analysis; that the making of decisions, because of the intricately linked nature of their consequences, will have an increasingly technical character. The husbanding of talent and the spread of educational and intellectual institutions will become a prime concern for the society; not only the best talents but eventually the entire complex of social prestige and social status will be rooted in the intellectual and scientific communities.[1]

Bell seems to feel that we are moving away from a system of individual choice toward a "communal ethic," with the political system rather than the free market becoming the mechanism for identifying goals and priorities.

Economist Robert Heilbroner provides another point of view. Noting that the persistence of severe social problems in the face of phenomenal growth over the past two decades demonstrates that economic success does not guarantee social harmony, he says this raises uncertainties about the future of capitalism and the corporation.

142

"It is possible," he adds, "that we stand at the threshold of an era in which deep-seated changes in lifeways will undermine capitalism in a manner as fatal as the most dramatic proletarian revolution might do, although perhaps less rapidly or romantically."

And Mr. Heilbroner then raises what I think is the ultimate challenge not only to business but to all American institutions:

> Throughout the globe, a long period of acquiescence before the fates is coming to an end. The passivity of the general run of men is waning. Where there was resignation, there is now impatience. Where there was acceptance, there is now the demand for control . . . The ultimate challenge to the institutions, motivations, political structures, lifeways and ideologies of capitalist nations is whether they can accommodate themselves to the requirements of a society in which an attitude of "social fatalism" is being replaced by one of social purpose.[2]

In my opinion, these are perceptive statements of the kinds of change that are occurring today and that will accelerate tomorrow. And they pose serious issues both for U.S. business and the nation.

For privately managed, investor-owned business, the basic issue is this: Can it continue to perceive, and adapt to, the changing needs and desires of people?

My experience and observation say unequivocally that it can. And that those who predict the decline of the corporation are seriously underestimating its ability not only to adapt to change but to initiate change in response to shifting circumstances. This has been true in regard to organization, management, human relationships, response to external pressures and the broadening of its view of its role in society. Business has, in short, participated in the research revolution and benefitted greatly from it.

Leonard S. Silk, chairman of the editorial board of *Business Week*, has affirmed the adaptability of business in another sense.

> American businesses have shown a remarkable ability to ride the trends of the times—to produce the instruments and tools of learning, loafing, calculation, reasoning, fighting, extending life and curbing fertility, traveling through space (inner and outer), or whatever it is the human race wants to do.[3]

The broader question for the nation is that of deciding what kind of economic system will serve it best in the future—private or government-directed enterprise. In looking at that question, we need to soberly consider both our past experience and the implications of permitting government to become the central force in economic affairs.

Among the points we must ponder are these: First, history has convincingly demonstrated that a private, incentive-oriented economic system, with all of its imperfections, is the system most compatible with the political freedom and individual liberty that are at the heart of the American experiment.

Second, our own experience in the past 100 years shows clearly that our system provides a variety of opportunity, a diversity of activity and a range of individual expression—all of which appear to be highly valued today by Americans, particularly young Americans—unequalled anywhere else in the world. And

144

third, our system has proved to be highly responsive to the changing desires of people, both on its own initiative and in responding to government initiatives.

If government is to supplant the free market as the central force in economic matters, we should anticipate a quite different future in each of these areas. For a government-directed economy means lessened freedom in all areas of our lives, homogenization and uniformity rather than diversity and individuality, and a system that is far less responsive to the needs of the individual.

The notion that direction of economic activity by elected representatives is a superior way of serving society's interests can be made to sound attractive in theory. But there is a considerable gap between theory and practice. And to illustrate that gap we need go no further than to contrast the operating performance of the nation's two communications giants, the U.S. Postal Service and the Bell System. For the financial difficulties and performance problems of the Postal Service contrast sharply with the record established by the Bell System in serving U.S. consumers.

The point is that there is little effective control over the state power of public enterprise. For that reason, it is less responsive to the public than is the private corporation that is tested daily in the marketplace. And because government decision-making is not subject to testing by competition, it has a potential for doing massive harm to the economy.

I believe that the supplanting of private enterprise by government as the central force in our economy would irreparably weaken the foundations of our entire political-economic system. *If* we wish to avoid that, we should concern ourselves today with using our system in the way it was designed to be used, through the provision of incentives to individual, private action. We need to think soberly also about providing new kinds of incentives—incentives which mirror the changing social and economic desires of the American people. The alternative to incentives is coercion, and a coercive system is not one that advances the condition of human society.

In conclusion, the future challenge to business is not unlike that facing America's other institutions: To take off the wraps, and use all of its resources and capabilities in a common effort to improve the quality of life for all. Essential to its doing so, however, is a better understanding between business and the society it serves.

We must seek of society a deeper knowledge of American business and what makes the system work, and judgments of business performance that are based on fact not myth. And we owe to society a keener perception of its needs, a bedrock *integrity* in meeting those needs and a communication job that explains understandably what we do—and how and why we do it. Past failures in these areas are at the root of the chief problems business is experiencing today.

As American business makes progress in these terms, it will indeed be meeting society's needs in a way that strengthens its ability to survive as a productive and self-renewing institution.

Reflections

—✳—

PEOPLE, PETROLEUM
AND PROGRESS

OVER the past four decades, I have been privileged to associate with people and participate in events that have impressed sharply upon me the nature of the forces that generate economic and social progress.

Chief among these forces in my experience are resourceful people willing to assume risks. A climate of freedom. Economic incentives. Wise and committed leadership. Clearly perceived goals. And a recognition of the supremacy of moral and spiritual values.

*

I was closely associated during much of my business career with J. Howard Pew and Joseph N. Pew, Jr., the two brothers who took over the management of Sun Oil Company upon the death of their father in 1912 and participated actively in its affairs for most of the next half-century.

Each in his own way symbolized the rugged individualism, the venturesomeness and the business acumen that characterized the men who built their small firms into the national and international companies that comprise the heart of American corporate enterprise today.

J. Howard Pew, who directed the company as president from 1912 until I succeeded him in 1947, was a many-sided man.

In business, he was an accomplished engineer, a skillful manager, a tough-minded taker of risks and an inspiring leader. Beyond business, his national identification with political conservatism reflected only one facet of his interests and activities. For he was also a true philanthropist, a champion of education, a committed Christian who was once characterized by Billy Graham as "one of the best informed laymen in America on the Bible" and a consistent fighter for individual and institutional freedom in economic and all other areas of life and living. All of these qualities were reflected in his business associations.

While I met Mr. Pew in 1933, my first close association with him came in 1937 in connection with economic studies relative to the commercial development of a catalytic refining process. And his role in that revolutionary venture well demonstrates the entrepreneurial vision and the technical capabilities and interests that were at the base of Sun's emergence as an industry leader in refining technology.

In the early 1930s, the French inventor, Eugene Houdry, was seeking financial support from U.S. companies for the development work necessary to perfect a catalytic process for "cracking" heavy fuels into the lighter petroleum fractions that make up gasoline. (At that time, gasoline production from crude oil was restricted to the amount available through normal distillation and thermal cracking processes.) Initially, the Socony-Vacuum Company (now Mobil) agreed to provide the financial backing Mr. Houdry sought. But, following the discovery of the giant East Texas oil field in 1931, and the resulting glut of low-cost crude, Mr. Houdry was advised to seek help elsewhere.

Mr. Pew, with the assistance of a nephew, Arthur E. Pew, Jr., an accomplished engineer and Sun manufacturing executive, reviewed the status of the research and decided that none of the problems standing in the way of commercial development were insurmountable. Under J. Howard's leadership, Sun's board quickly decided to back Mr. Houdry with financial and research assistance. And with Arthur Pew, and Sun engineers including Clarence H. Thayer, playing a leading role, the Houdry process was perfected and the world's first commercial plant was completed at Sun's Marcus Hook, Pa., refinery in 1937.

Shortly thereafter, that process made possible the supply of high-octane aviation fuels to Britain in the critical early days of World War II, and subsequently fueled the Allied air war. And the concept of catalytic refining born with the Houdry development is at the base of today's high-volume production of high-octane fuels.

Testifying also to Mr. Pew's farsightedness was his strong support in his later years for Sun's participation in the pioneering venture that resulted in 1967 in the world's first commercial production of synthetic crude oil from Canada's vast Athabasca tar sands.

In the early 1960s, Great Canadian Oil Sands Limited, the company spearheading the tar sands development project, began to run into money problems. Promised financial support began to erode in the face of severe technological challenges posed by mining and processing problems, and in the light of the wide availability and low price of conventional oil. By 1964, Sun was the last remaining hope for the project, and the company faced the hard question of substantial direct investment in a foreign nation. In wrestling with a decision, the company's board of directors had to consider troublesome questions relating to competition from conventional oil, highly uncertain profit prospects and the possibility of extremely heavy future financial requirements. In the board's deliberations, Mr. Pew argued strongly for direct involvement. His view prevailed and the project went forward on the strength of an initial direct commitment of $67.5 million by Sun.

The oil flowing from the Athabasca sands today is in large measure a testimonial to Mr. Pew's vision. And the potential opened up by that initial development looms ever larger in the light of worldwide energy scarcity.

Part and parcel of Mr. Pew's make-up was his conviction that the strength of the American enterprise system lay in the freedom it provided for private initiative and vigorous competition. This was reflected in one of my earliest close associations with him, back in 1939. At that time, I assisted him in the preparation of testimony for presentation to the Temporary National Economic Committee which was investigating economic concentration in America. And I recall him expressing his views then in these words:

> We have never assumed a divine right to a place and a share in the petroleum industry. If somebody else could serve the public better in quality or in price, he was entitled to the business. . . . It has been a case of root hog or die, and my agricultural friends tell me that the most vigorous rooter is usually the healthiest hog. . . . The industry has become what it is under a regime of free enterprise and wide-open competition, with little government interference.[1]

That commitment to freedom never wavered. And in later years, he frequently made this point:

> When a people come to look upon their government as a source of all their rights, there will surely come a time when they will look upon that same government as the source of all their wrongs. . . . Freedom is indivisible. Once industrial freedom is lost, political freedom, religious freedom and freedom of the press and of speech will all fall.[2]

Joseph N. Pew, Jr., was an equally astute business thinker and played a key role in shaping Sun Oil Company. After 35 years as a Sun vice president, he became board chairman in 1947 when I was elected to the presidency. Working with him was a unique and enriching experience, and I remain impressed to this day by his prophetic business vision and his depth of human understanding.

No "fuss and feathers" man, to use his own words, he was not impressed by formalized management techniques. He was immensely practical and down-to-earth, a pragmatist who had an exceptional ability to go right to the heart of a problem and act decisively.

Reflecting that pragmatic approach, he played a major role as idea man in such major undertakings as the establishing of Sun Shipbuilding and Dry Dock Company as a Sun subsidiary during World War I, the company's pioneering product pipeline operations in the early 1930s, and in needling its research and marketing departments into the development of the Custom Blending gasoline marketing system introduced in 1956.

Much more active politically than his brother, Howard, he was equally strong in his conviction that business must remain free of unnecessary government restraint. On Sun's 75th Anniversary in 1961, he expressed his philosophy in these words:

> Deep within Sun Oil during these 75 years has been the conviction that the sole alternative to freedom of competition is a government-directed economy, and that such a substitute for the competition of a free marketplace eventually would end all freedom. . . . We likewise believe that America's greatest resource and strength is the resourcefulness of free men, with opportunities and incentives that encourage them to take risks and work diligently to improve their economic condition through serving their fellow men better than others do.[3]

Together, the Pew brothers provided a unique combination of the talents that made possible the shaping of a small regional oil company into a major national and international energy corporation, developing fuel resources around the world, providing productive employment to 25,000 people and serving an ever-expanding circle of customers with a growing variety of useful products. They were resourceful, purposeful, practical, far-seeing businessmen keenly sensitive to their responsibilities to employees, stockholders and customers, and deeply committed to the private enterprise system. They were responsive to an economic environment that provided opportunities for growth and incentives to growth. They were socially responsible, before "social responsibility" in business became the fashionable term that it is today. They were men of unquestioned integrity. And they built an organization that has been increasingly of broader service to society.

*

The Athabasca tar sands development project which J. Howard Pew so staunchly supported was one of the most unusual and significant projects that Sun was involved in during my years in executive management.

Its uniqueness and significance derived from these basic characteristics:

It was the first all-out assault on a major energy resource that had defied all previous development efforts, and a completely new venture in synthetic fuels production.

It required starting from scratch in a frontier area completely foreign to industrial development.

It required the risking of large amounts of capital in a venture rife with uncertainty.

It required the cooperative efforts of the business and government institutions of two great nations.

155

And, perhaps above all, it offered the exciting opportunity of a completely new venture, one that if successful would make contributions far beyond the immediate impact on petroleum supply to serving the energy needs of the people of North America and the world.

An estimated 250 billion barrels of recoverable oil are locked in the vast tar sands deposits that sprawl across 30,000 acres of Alberta Province. Of primary importance is that portion of the Athabasca sands suitable for open-pit mining, which is expected to yield 26.5 billion barrels of oil. Standing between these raw resources and usable fuel was the complex task of removing a heavy overburden of earth and rock to get at the oil-impregnated sand, mining the sands in a continuous flow operation, extracting the heavy bitumen, processing that into a clean synthetic fuel and getting it to market. And adding to these considerable problems was the remoteness of the area and the bitterly cold climate with temperatures ranging down to 60 degrees below zero.

Sun's interest in the puzzle of the tar sands goes back to the mid-1940s when the company first began to consider the feasibility of synthetic fuel production there. In 1954, we secured a 75 percent interest in the lease that was destined to become the site of the first commercial operations. And late in the 1950s we contracted with a Canadian firm, Great Canadian Oil Sands Limited, to take 75 percent of the output from a plant to be built on our lease. We did not then anticipate investing directly in the venture.

Approval for construction of a 31,500 barrels daily plant (later increased to 45,000 barrels daily) was obtained by GCOS from the Alberta government in 1962 and preliminary construction activities got under way in 1963.

After GCOS ran into financing difficulties and Sun committed itself to direct investment, the project moved into the actual construction stage in 1964.

Construction of the extraction and processing facilities and the assembling of equipment for overburden removal and mining operations required three years, running into the summer of 1967. It involved the solution of complex logistical problems, as well as advances in mining and extraction technology. At the peak of construction activity, the work-force numbered over 2,300 people, composed of individuals from every province and territory in Canada and from many foreign nations, with a wide variety of skills and capabilities.

The project required the massing of equipment and supplies from literally around the globe, and moving that mass more than 250 miles from the supply jump-off in the city of Edmonton to the plant site near the frontier village of Fort McMurray. Beyond the plant and mining facilities, the job also entailed the building of a pipeline to Edmonton to get the synthetic crude to market, and the construction of new housing and other facilities in Fort McMurray for the initial plant force of some 700 people.

By mid-summer 1967, Canada's centennial year, the extraction and processing facilities were in place, the giant bucketwheel excavators from West Germany that would dig up to 140,000 tons of oil sand daily were assembled, the pipeline was completed and the complex was ready to go. It was formally dedicated in

September, representing at that time a total investment of some $250 million, the largest private investment in the history of Canada.

But it represented something more, too, and that was the unlocking of a vast new energy resource for man's use. Beyond the physical and technological problems that had to be licked to achieve this, the varied contributions of many people in Canada and the United States were vitally important. High on this list were J. Howard Pew and the then chief executive of Alberta, its distinguished premier, Ernest C. Manning.

By 1967, Mr. Manning had presided over and played a major role in the rise of Alberta from poverty to riches. A cabinet minister at age 26, and elected premier in 1943 at age 35, he went on to win nine consecutive elections over a period of 24 years, heading what *Time* magazine once called "the nearest approach to a theocracy in the Western Hemisphere."

An inspiring leader, skilled administrator and deeply religious man who has long been a Baptist lay preacher, Ernest Manning was committed to the development of Alberta's resources for the benefit of Alberta's people. And, in accordance with his support for the private enterprise system, he wisely provided incentives for private capital investment, while at the same time judiciously protecting the interests of Albertans.

Premier Manning and J. Howard Pew were in many ways alike, and held each other in high regard. Both were featured speakers at the dedication ceremonies for the Athabasca facilities in September 1967.

Although there was no worry about impending oil shortage in that year, Mr. Pew's remarks reflected the foresight that marked his entire career. He said then, in part:

> No nation can long be secure in this atomic age unless it is amply supplied with petroleum. The best minds in the oil industry estimate that by 1985 the world's requirements for petroleum will be 2½ times what they are today; and for the North American continent, they estimate that by 1985 the demand will be twice the present consumption. It is the considered opinion of our group that if the North American continent is to produce the oil to meet its requirements in the years ahead, oil from the Athabasca area must of necessity play an important role.[4]

Premier Manning, in turn, spoke to the essential purpose of resource development, expressing his thoughts in these words:

> Behind every worthwhile industrial project there must be a worthwhile purpose or motivating objective. That objective must be to produce something that man needs for the enhancement of his progress and his well-being on earth. And to this end there must be on the part of industry a constant striving to achieve this objective and, in the process, to attain an even higher standard of excellence. In this province, we are dedicated to the proposition that physical resource development must always have as its foremost purpose the development of the human resources of the province and nation. This purpose is not merely to provide mankind with a higher standard of material living, but *to create the social and economic conditions under which free and creative men and women can best develop their individual talents, fulfill their hopes and aspirations and make their personal dreams come*

true. With this objective in mind, it is fitting
that we gather here today to dedicate this plant
not merely to the production of oil but to the
continual progress and enrichment of mankind.[5]

*

My involvement in the venture that led to construction of a Sun refinery in Puerto Rico late in the
1960s provided from a somewhat different perspective
additional evidence of the impact that productive
investment of capital can have on people and their
economic and social situation.

In the 1930s, Puerto Rico was an impoverished land
with a limited industrial capability and an unpromis-
ing future to offer its people. Since then the island
has undergone an economic transformation that is
little short of miraculous. This is reflected today in
scores of new industrial development projects, a growing number of new plants, an expanding production
capability and a rising standard of living.

The thrust of this expansion came through the government Industrial Development Company—widely
known as Fomento—established in 1942. Initially,
this agency concentrated on direct government participation in production, and substantial progress was
gained. In 1948, however, initiation of the famed
"Operation Bootstrap" provided a new private thrust,
and industrial expansion went into high gear.

Rather than government directly participating,
money and effort then began to be directed toward
energizing private business and speeding up the flow
of private capital into productive investment. Government began to focus on spurring private initiative, in

other words, through identifying important investment opportunities and guiding private investors to them.

Those efforts have paid off. From 1950 to the early 1970s, gross product rose from $755 million to about $6 billion and per capita income increased six-fold. And the annual growth rate was continuing to exceed 10 percent.

These gains reflect the able leadership provided by Puerto Rico's government officials, many of whom I have been privileged to deal with personally, and their commitment to incentive-oriented economic policies.

Former governor Luis Munoz Marin provided the initial political impetus for the island's economic turnaround back in the 1940s and early 1950s. And momentum created then has been ably maintained by Luis A. Ferre, governor from 1969 to 1972, and the present governor, Rafael Hernandez Colon.

At the implementation level, the prime mover in the island's economic leap forward has been Theodoro (Ted) Moscoso, who was named the first administrator of the Economic Development Company back in 1942. He filled that post until named ambassador to Venezuela by President Kennedy in 1961; and, after distinguished service in other public and private posts, he was called back to Fomento by Governor Hernandez Colon early in 1973.

The imaginative administration provided by Ambassador Moscoso, Rafael Durand and Sergio Camero, both former Fomento administrators, and others has been a major factor in the island's progress.

In more recent years, the focus of Fomento has shifted to the development of capital intensive industries that build a solid industrial base, with particular emphasis on petroleum refining and petrochemicals. As a part of this expansion, we in Sun Oil Company have participated directly in the economic development of the island.

This participation grew out of our decision in 1968 to build a refinery in Puerto Rico, primarily to expand our lubricating oil production through the use of foreign crude oil. We broke ground in 1969 for a 66,000 barrels per day plant and a $15 million all-weather port. These facilities were completed in 1970, and the refinery has since been expanded to 85,000 barrels daily.

Our refinery, located in Yabucoa on the southeast corner of the island, has had a substantial impact upon the community. A town of 30,000 people, Yabucoa has traditionally been an agricultural area, with seasonal employment, substantial unemployment and relatively low incomes. More recently, its situation has been improving under the island's economic development program, and Sun's refinery has been playing a major role in this. Our investment of some $125 million in the project has provided jobs for more than 400 people, and created an annual payroll of $4 million—the highest in Yabucoa's history.

This is not a new phenomenon for Puerto Rico. It has occurred again and again, resulting in an economic transformation that has generated jobs, higher incomes and a rising standard of living for a growing number of Puerto Ricans, and a solid industrial base that promises greater progress for more people in the future.

*

Reflections: People, Petroleum and Progress

My experiences as chairman of the board of the American Petroleum Institute in 1966 and 1967 deeply impressed upon me the role that the American petroleum industry has played in industrial development in the United States.

I found then that I had never before truly recognized the vastness of the industry's resources, the complexities of its operations, the capabilities of its people and the essentiality of its services to life today.

Beyond its U.S. operations, it has carried petroleum technology around the world, playing a major role in finding and bringing to market most of the world's oil.

In 1967, as A.P.I. chairman, I represented the U.S. petroleum industry at the Seventh World Petroleum Congress in Mexico City. My participation in meetings and discussions there with representatives of virtually every Free World nation and the Soviet Union pointed up sharply the international flavor of petroleum operations. The emphasis placed on sharing information across national boundaries, discussing common problems and jointly assessing the future demonstrated to me a level of international cooperation that I think is unique on the industrial scene today.

In representing Sun, I have had firsthand knowledge of international petroleum operations and their impact on both underdeveloped and developed nations. One was the 1968 dedication of the Sassan Field in the Persian Gulf, found and produced by an international consortium including Sun, where the Iranian government recognized the role played by American firms in developing this new source of petroleum supply.

Another example was the opening of new facilities at Bacton, England, in 1969, for handling natural gas produced in the North Sea. The new supplies of gas, from the Hewett Field found and produced by a group of American companies including Sun, were referred to then by the British Gas Council as "playing a fundamental role in ushering in an era of great economic opportunity for Britain."

Still another example is the contribution of the petroleum industry to the economic development of Venezuela, where Sun has been a major producer since it brought in the rich Lake Maracaibo field in 1957. Revenues from oil taxes and royalties, which provide more than half of the Venezuelan government's income, have sparked a major economic advance. And while many do not yet share in that advance, progress can be seen throughout the country in new schools, homes, businesses, cultural institutions and health facilities.

*

Where I have observed large achievements in industry and industrial development, I have observed also the presence of a high order of leadership provided by committed individuals. And this has frequently reminded me of a comment by J. Douglas Brown, former Princeton University professor, who wrote:

> The image of a leader is not his superficial self, but rather the personification of a system of values which he has demonstrated over time.
>
> Human understanding, introspection, intuitive integrity, a sense of total responsibility, courage, decisiveness, a desire for accomplishment and a

style of his own—these are the fundamental attributes of a leader of human beings.[6]

Professor Brown goes on to say that when this manifestation of leadership reflects "a quality of personal integrity," it is a powerful instrument. And my experience suggests that this is, indeed, true.

On the world scene, I think of Sir Winston Churchill, with whom I once shared a three-hour luncheon conversation. During the course of that conversation, which ranged over Mr. Churchill's experiences in government, his aspirations for the British people and the gamut of international petroleum issues, the qualities of leadership which he embodied came through quite clearly—particularly his innate courage, his decisiveness and his unique and magnetic personal style.

The leadership provided by Premier Ernest Manning in advancing the interests of the people of Alberta Province through resource development reflects an overriding commitment to accomplishment and a sense of total responsibility for the government tasks entrusted to him. Other examples from my personal experience include Martin Meyerson, in directing, as president, the affairs of the University of Pennsylvania; and the Reverend Leon Sullivan, who has shown outstanding leadership and dedication in providing training and vocational opportunities for the disadvantaged in a hundred cities across the country and overseas.

J. Howard Pew, in my long assocation with him, reflected an identifiable and enduring "system of values" in the very highest sense of the concept. Chief among these were integrity, human understanding and a deep commitment to high moral and ethical standards.

Above all, Mr. Pew symbolized personal integrity, to the point that even those who disagreed with him most violently never questioned the sincerity of his commitment to the principles he espoused. This was impressed upon me during one of my earliest associations with him, when I accompanied him to Washington, D.C., to testify before the temporary National Economic Committee. At the conclusion of his statement, a member of Congress, visibly impressed, approached me with this comment: "You know," he said, "your boss not only speaks like an affidavit, he looks like one."

Mr. Pew succeeded in investing the Sun organization with his style of leadership. And the company continues to benefit today from that legacy in terms of the attention accorded to its views on public issues involving energy considerations.

*

A quality common to successful leaders, it seems to me, is the recognition of a spiritual force in life transcending the human condition. And it is my experience that such a recognition is fundamental to all productive actions and relationships.

Recent events in our country have pointed up rather dramatically the personal and institutional dilemmas that can arise when those in leadership capacities fail to recognize overriding moral and ethical precepts. This was demonstrated in the business community by the actions of a small number of companies in making illegal political contributions in the 1972 presidential campaign, actions which seriously damaged the credibility of business generally.

166

It is my observation that the lack of guiding spiritual and moral values today is reflected in a growing national uncertainty and confusion, a vague sense of dissatisfaction with things as they are and a lack of direction and purpose in making them better. These individual feelings are, in turn, reflected in the stances of our political, economic and social institutions.

Samuel Stiles, a Scottish author of the nineteenth century, once wrote that moral qualities rule the world. I think that is precisely true. And this suggests to me that our nation today needs to recommit itself to some old values.

One is recommitment to belief in a Creator who is sovereign in the affairs of men and nations.

A second is recommitment to a set of moral values that has been the root of our strength in the past, but that too often receives only lip-service in the present— and that in the minds of many apparently has been consigned to oblivion in the anticipated future. This moral or spiritual stance is a blend of the concepts of love, humility, justice, compassion, trust and responsibility. These are the qualities that are the essence of productive day-to-day relationships among people. They add up to a moral posture that is highly demanding of the individual, because it is based squarely on the concept of personal responsibility. It reflects the conviction that man is guided by will, not driven by instinct.

John Gardner has made this point very aptly. If, he said, the individual "is to avoid becoming a moral cripple, he must refuse to divest himself of moral responsibility for his acts." And he added this warning: "A people who hand moral responsibility over to society will eventually have their impulses brought under control by society."

A third is recommitment to the concept of life under law, and the accompanying axiom that change be effectuated through lawful processes. We are today at a considerable distance from this concept in the actions that are contemplated and undertaken by many in our country.

Several years ago, I was involved in a dialogue, as a member of the board of trustees of the University of Pennsylvania, with members of the faculty in regard to the University's position on student dissent. I expressed the view that students should be encouraged to work for change through established processes built into our form of government for this express purpose. And I remember as a part of this dialogue one professor's comment that "the rule of law is the cement of society."

The fact that some of the brickwork of our society is crumbling around us today is a measure of the extent to which we have ignored or given only lip-service to the rule of law.

A fourth is recommitment to the concept of the brotherhood of man—the essential oneness that John Donne expressed when he wrote "no man is an island entire of itself; every man is a piece of the continent, a part of the main. . . ."

One of the saddest and potentially most damaging developments of our day is the growing divisiveness among us. This is due in part, I think, to both real and imagined injustices of the past and present, in part to an overemphasis on the possession of material things and in part to the efforts of those who promote conflict as a means of seeking their own ends. Whatever the reason, such division strikes at the very essence of the commonality of interests upon which our way of life is built.

I am reminded of the words spoken by Benjamin Franklin during the tense deliberations surrounding the drafting of our Constitution. He said:

> In this situation of this assembly, groping in the dark as it were to find political truth, and scarce able to distinguish it when presented to us, how has it happened, sir, that we have not hitherto once thought of humbly applying to the Father of lights to illuminate our understanding . . . ?
>
> I have lived, sir, a long time, and the longer I live the more convincing proofs I see of this truth—that God governs in the affairs of men. . . .
>
> We have been assured, sir, in the Sacred writings, that except the Lord build the house, they labor in vain that build it. I firmly believe this; and I also believe that without his concurring aid, we shall succeed in this political building no better than the builders of Babel.[7]

We are again today "groping in the dark." And the light of understanding lies along the same route that Mr. Franklin pointed out to our forefathers some 200 years ago.

Notes

PART I

Chapter 1

1. Max Ways, "Finding the American Direction," *Fortune*, October 1970, p. 126.
2. William Letwin, "The Past and Future of the American Businessman," *Daedalus*, Winter 1969, p. 17.
3. Max Ways, "Business Needs to Do a Better Job of Explaining Itself," *Fortune*, September 1972, p. 192.
4. John F. Mee, *Management Thought in a Dynamic Economy* (New York: New York University Press, 1963), p. 110.

Chapter 2

1. David E. Lilienthal, *Management: A Humanist Art* (New York: Columbia University Press, 1967), pp. 32-33.
2. Edwin J. Singer and John Ramsden, *Human Resources— Obtaining Results from People at Work* (London: McGraw-Hill, 1972), p. 181.
3. S. I. Hayakawa, quoted in H. R. Sharbaugh, "Unleash the People," *Vital Speeches*, April 15, 1971, p. 415.

170

4. H. R. Sharbaugh, president, Sun Oil Company, in an address before the American Institute of Chemical Engineers, Houston, Texas, March 1, 1971.
5. M. Scott Myers, *Every Employee a Manager* (New York: McGraw-Hill, 1970), p. xii.

Chapter 3

1. Daniel Yankelovich, Inc., *Corporate Priorities, 1973* (New York, 1973), p. 1 (a report to sponsoring companies).
2. E. B. Weiss, "Marketers Fiddle While Consumers Burn," *Harvard Business Review*, July-August 1968, p. 48.
3. *New York Times*, January 21, 1974, p. 37.
4. V. O. Marquez, "Corporate Enterprise—Its Social, Economic and Political Environment," *Vital Speeches*, October 15, 1972, p. 17.

Chapter 4

1. *Wall Street Journal*, January 23, 1974, p. 12.
2. George Cabot Lodge, "Top Priority: Renovating Our Ideology," *Harvard Business Review*, September-October 1970, p. 50.
3. Lee Loevinger, "Social Responsibility in a Democratic Society," *Vital Speeches*, April 15, 1973, p. 393.

PART II

Chapter 5

1. Committee for Economic Development, *Social Responsibilities of Business Corporations* (New York, 1971), pp. 14, 16.
2. John Diebold, an address before Ministry of Economics and Finance Meeting, Paris, France, June 21, 1972.
3. *Wall Street Journal*, December 26, 1973, p. 4.
4. Max Ways, "Business Needs to Do a Better Job of Explaining Itself," *Fortune*, September 1972, p. 196.
5. C. Jackson Grayson, "Let's Get Back to the Competitive Market System," *Harvard Business Review*, November-December 1973, p. 108.

Chapter 6

1. Harris Survey report, quoted in *OUR SUN* (Sun Oil Company), Summer 1973, p. 14.
2. Milton Friedman, *Capitalism and Freedom* (Chicago: University of Chicago Press, 1962), p. 133.
3. Adam Smith, *An Inquiry Into the Nature and Causes of the Wealth of Nations* (Chicago: Encyclopaedia Britannica, Inc., 1952), p. 194.
4. Daniel Yankelovich, quoted in Philip Drotning, "Why Nobody Takes Corporate Social Responsibility Seriously," *Business and Society Review*, Autumn 1972, p. 72.

Chapter 7

1. Dennis L. Meadows and others, *The Limits to Growth* (New York: Universe Books, 1972), p. 183.
2. E. J. Mishan, "The Limits of Abundance" (essay in the America and the Future of Man series), University of California, 1973.
3. Mancur Olson, "Introduction to the No-Growth Society," *Daedalus*, Fall 1973, p. 8.
4. Valery Giscard d'Estaing, quoted in address by John Diebold before Ministry of Economics and Finance Meeting, Paris, France, June 21, 1972.

Part III

Chapter 8

1. Allan Nevins in *Energy and Man—A Symposium* (New York: Appleton-Century-Crofts, Inc., 1960), pp. 6, 7.
2. Robert G. Dunlop in *Energy and Man—A Symposium* (New York: Appleton-Century-Crofts, Inc., 1960), p. 42-43.

Chapter 9

1. Robert G. Dunlop, president, Sun Oil Company, in an address before the Independent Petroleum Association of America, Houston, Texas, October 30, 1967.

Chapter 10

1. U.S. Department of the Interior, *United States Energy —A Summary Review* (Washington, D.C.: 1972), p. 2.

Notes

2. M. A. Adelman, "Energy, A Complex Mass of Problems," *Vital Speeches*, June 15, 1973, p. 518.

Part IV

1. Daniel Bell, "Notes on the Post-Industrial Society," *The Public Interest*, Winter 1967, p. 30.
2. Robert L. Heilbroner, "The Future of Capitalism," *World*, September 12, 1972, p. 30.
3. Leonard S. Silk, "Business Power Today and Tomorrow," *Daedalus*, Winter 1969, p. 187.

Reflections

1. J. Howard Pew in "Investigation of Concentration of Economic Power," hearings of the Temporary National Economic Committee, Washington, D.C., September 26, 1939, pp. 7,174.
2. J. Howard Pew, collected speeches, Sun Oil Company, St. Davids, Pa.
3. Joseph N. Pew, Jr., "Faith in Free Markets," *OUR SUN*, Summer-Autumn 1961, p. 2.
4. J. Howard Pew, chairman, Sun Oil Company, in an address delivered at Fort McMurray, Alberta, Canada, September 30, 1967.
5. Ernest C. Manning, premier, Alberta Province, in an address delivered at Fort McMurray, Alberta, Canada, September 30, 1967.
6. J. Douglas Brown, "The Attributes of the Effective Leader," *University: A Princeton Quarterly*, Fall 1973, pp. 19, 20.
7. Benjamin Franklin, as reported by James Madison, *Documents Illustrative of the Formation of the Union of the American States* (Government Printing Office: Washington, D.C., 1927), pp. 295-296.